PRACTICAL AI FOR BEGINNERS

UNLOCK THE POWER OF ARTIFICIAL INTELLIGENCE WITH SIMPLE TOOLS TO BOOST PRODUCTIVITY, SAVE TIME, AND MAKE SMARTER DECISIONS IN EVERYDAY LIFE

PACO BARKER

CONTENTS

INTRODUCTION

In our rapidly evolving world, the demand for efficiency is greater than ever, making it essential to find smarter ways to work. The pressure to stay productive can often feel overwhelming, but this is where artificial intelligence (AI) makes a difference. No longer just a concept of the future, AI is already reshaping how we work and navigate daily life. From automating repetitive tasks to helping us make better decisions, AI has the power to enhance efficiency and streamline the activities we do every day.

But here's the thing: you don't need to be a tech expert or a computer scientist to harness the benefits. That's why I wrote this book, *Practical AI for Beginners: Unlock the Power of Artificial Intelligence with Simple Tools to Boost Productivity, Save Time, and Make Smarter Decisions in Everyday Life.* Whether you're a beginner or someone without a technical background, my goal is to equip you with the knowledge to understand and apply AI in ways that help you get what you want—whether that's reducing stress, improving work performance, keeping up with the latest trends, or simply making everyday tasks easier.

This book is not about promoting any specific tools or technologies. Instead, I'll introduce various AI-powered tools and examples for reference—so you can then decide what works best for you. My focus is on practical applications, showing you how to integrate AI into your daily life without adding unnecessary complications.

One of the most accessible and powerful AI tools today is ChatGPT. That's why I've dedicated an entire chapter to it, guiding you step by step on how to start using the platform right away. You'll learn how to leverage it for tasks like research, writing, and even getting personalized assistance—whether you need help drafting emails, generating creative ideas, or planning your next vacation. More importantly, you'll discover how to craft effective prompts that unlock ChatGPT's full potential, helping you get the most accurate and useful responses.

Beyond simply using AI, we'll also discuss important ethical considerations, including transparency, accountability, and privacy. I've also included a chapter on identifying AI-generated content, which is an increasingly relevant skill in today's digital landscape. With AI playing a larger role in media, work, and everyday interactions, it is crucial to recognize what's real, what's synthetic, and what that means for society.

By the end of this book, you will feel more comfortable and less intimidated by AI, equipped with the skills to use common AI tools and an understanding of fundamental concepts. You will see how AI can enhance your productivity, save time, and support better decision-making across various aspects of both your personal and professional life.

Now, I know what you might be thinking. Is AI really for me? Could it eventually replace my job? Is it safe? All of which are valid concerns, and I'm here to address them head-on. This book will debunk common myths and provide a balanced perspective on AI's role in our lives. AI isn't here to replace you—it's here to empower you, helping you work smarter and achieve your goals with less effort.

So, are you ready to embark on this journey of discovery? Are you ready to unlock the power of AI and transform your everyday life? If so, then let's dive in. I encourage you to actively engage with the content, explore the tools, and see for yourself how AI can make a difference. Together, we'll take this journey one step at a time.

1

UNDERSTANDING THE BASICS OF AI

Welcome to the exciting world of AI! Once considered a concept of science fiction, AI is now a reality that influences many aspects of our daily lives—from how we shop and navigate to how we communicate and work. But what exactly is AI? This chapter will explain the core concepts, presenting them in a straightforward and easy-to-understand manner. By the end, you'll have an understanding of the basic frameworks of AI and why this technology is continuing to shape the world around us.

WHAT IS AI?

Artificial intelligence, or AI, is more than a term tossed around in tech circles. It's a fascinating field where machines mimic human cognitive functions (i.e., learning, reasoning, and problem-solving). Picture a digital brain that can process information, make decisions, and even improve itself over time. The capability of machines to simulate human-like thinking is transforming the way we engage with technology. At its core, AI is built to create systems that perform tasks once thought to require human intellect. From identifying patterns and forecasting outcomes to interpreting language, AI is designed to mirror human thought processes and behaviors in increasingly sophisticated ways.

The technology works by processing vast amounts of data and identifying patterns within it. Let's break this down into four simple steps:

1. **Data Collection** – AI needs information to learn. This could be anything from pictures of cats and dogs to words and sentences in different languages.
2. **Pattern Recognition** – AI then looks for similarities and differences in the data. For example, it can learn to recognize the difference between a cat and a dog by analyzing thousands of pictures.
3. **Decision Making** – Once it understands patterns, AI can make predictions or decisions. For example, a self-driving car can decide when to stop, turn, or speed up based on traffic patterns.
4. **Learning and Improving** – AI improves over time by learning from mistakes and new experiences, much like a human would.

To make this more relatable, think of AI as a helpful assistant in your daily life. Just like a personal assistant who manages your schedule, reminds you of tasks, and keeps track of your plans, AI works behind the scenes to streamline your activities. For example, it can sort through your emails, prioritize important messages, and filter out spam, freeing up your time for more meaningful work. AI simplifies complex processes, making everyday tasks more efficient while personalizing your experiences to better suit your needs.

However, despite its capabilities, it's fair to say that AI is often misunderstood. A common misconception is that the technology might end up becoming self-aware like humans. But unlike humans, who learn from experiences, intuition, and emotions, AI operates purely on logic and pattern recognition. It cannot reason abstractly, form opinions, or make moral decisions. Simply put, AI's intelligence is narrow. While it excels in specific tasks like chess or data analysis, it lacks self-reflection, ingenuity, and true understanding—the hallmarks of human intelligence.

CORE CONCEPTS AND TERMINOLOGY

Let's now take a closer look at the fundamental concepts of AI, shedding light on the technologies and methodologies that drive it. By understanding these core ideas, you'll gain a clearer picture of how AI systems work and the principles that guide their operations. This foundational knowledge will help you see beyond the buzzwords and grasp the true potential of AI.

It's important to understand that AI isn't just one technology —it's a collection of powerful techniques that enable machines to learn, reason, and adapt. Key methodologies include machine learning, neural networks, deep learning, and natural language processing (NLP). We'll explore these concepts in more detail to uncover how they shape the world of AI.

Machine Learning

Machine learning is the foundational branch of AI that empowers computers to analyze data, identify patterns, and make decisions without needing explicit programming for each task. Unlike traditional programming, where rules and instructions are predefined, machine learning systems identify patterns in data and refine their performance over time. This ability to adapt and learn is what makes AI so powerful in fields such as healthcare, finance, and automation.

Machine learning is built on algorithms, which are step-by-step instructions that help computers analyze data, identify patterns, and make predictions. Think of an algorithm as a recipe that guides AI in recognizing trends. The process begins by feeding data into the algorithm, which then analyzes the information before making adjustments based on what it learns. With each cycle of learning and refinement, the model becomes more accurate, leading to increasingly reliable decisions.

Machine learning features three fundamental types that utilize distinct methods for specialized applications.

- **Supervised Learning** is the most common type of AI learning, where a model is trained using examples that already have correct answers. Think of it like a teacher showing a student flashcards with both a picture and the correct label. For example, in a dog breed identification app, the AI is given pictures of dogs (inputs) along with their breed names (labels). By studying a number of labeled examples, the model learns to recognize patterns and associate specific features with each breed. Once trained, it can then look at a new dog picture and predict its breed based on what it has learned. This approach is widely used in applications such as spam detection in emails and handwriting recognition.
- **Unsupervised Learning** is different because it doesn't use labeled data—meaning the AI isn't given the "right answers." Instead, it explores the data on its own and looks for patterns or groups. Imagine being given a pile of puzzle pieces without knowing the final picture—you'd start grouping similar pieces together based on color or shape. A real-world example is identifying different types of shoppers based on their buying habits, without knowing their

specific preferences in advance. Unsupervised learning uncovers hidden patterns and relationships within data that may not be immediately apparent.

- **Reinforcement Learning** works through a system of rewards and penalties, much like training a pet. The AI tries different actions and learns from the results—good choices get rewarded, while bad ones receive negative feedback. For instance, an autonomous vehicle adjusting its path in real time using sensors would receive positive feedback when it successfully avoids obstacles and negative feedback when it does not. This method is often used in robotics and game-playing AI, like the algorithms behind self-learning chess engines.

Neural Networks

Neural networks process data through multiple interconnected layers of artificial "neurons" that emulate the human brain's structure. These networks are particularly good at tasks like image and speech recognition. An example you are likely familiar with would be a neural network helping your phone recognize your face when you unlock it using facial recognition.

At their core, neural networks consist of three main layers: the input layer, hidden layers, and the output layer. The input layer receives raw data, such as pixels from an image or words from a text. The hidden layers act as the network's computational engine, identifying patterns and features by adjusting weighted connections during training. Finally, the output layer translates these learned patterns into meaningful predictions or classifications.

Neural networks learn through training, a process where they continuously refine their internal settings to improve accuracy. The network makes a prediction, compares it to the correct answer, and adjusts its settings to reduce errors. This cycle repeats thousands or even millions of times, allowing the network to gradually improve its performance over time. Unlike traditional machine learning, which requires humans to manually define important features, neural networks automatically discover patterns, making them especially powerful for handling unstructured data such as images, speech, and natural language.

Deep Learning

This is a more advanced type of neural network that can process extensive amounts of data through multiple layers. Deep learning enables highly complex operations like translating languages, diagnosing diseases from medical images, and generating text that resembles human writing. Deep learning stands out in its capability to process large quantities of unstructured data, such as images, audio files, and text-based information without substantial human involvement.

Natural Language Processing (NLP)

NLP allows computers to process human language and provide meaningful responses. This technology drives functionality in chatbots, virtual assistants, and language translation tools. When you ask your smart speaker for the weather or type a question into a search engine, NLP helps it understand and process your request.

NLP also includes technologies like:

- **Sentiment Analysis** – AI can determine the emotional tone behind a piece of text, helping businesses analyze customer feedback.
- **Speech Recognition** – Converts spoken language into text, used in voice assistants like Siri and Alexa.
- **Text Generation** – AI can generate human-like text, such as news articles or chatbot responses.

How These AI Technologies Are Related

Rather than functioning as separate, standalone tools, these AI technologies form a layered system. Machine learning is the groundwork, providing the ability for computers to recognize patterns in data and improve their accuracy over time. Neural networks build on machine learning by structuring these pattern-recognition tasks in interconnected layers, allowing AI to learn increasingly intricate features. When those layers become especially deep, we call it deep learning, which enables the analysis of vast, unstructured datasets with minimal human guidance.

NLP then leverages these deep learning techniques to understand and generate human language. The same neural networks that classify images or predict trends can also analyze sentence structure, interpret context, and produce meaningful responses. By combining machine learning, neural networks, deep learning, and NLP, AI systems can tackle a wide range of tasks—from language translation to driving cars—all by applying these technologies in tandem. Furthermore, these complementary developments are driving the next wave of AI innovation, culminating in generative AI, which we will now explore further.

INTRODUCTION TO GENERATIVE AI

You may have heard the term "Generative AI" in the news or on social media, but what does it really mean, and why should you care? Well, generative AI represents a major technological breakthrough that allows machines to produce new content across multiple formats such as text, images, music, and code. Generative AI goes beyond traditional AI approaches which concentrate on pattern recognition and decision-making by generating completely new data.

Generative AI operates through deep learning models which rely heavily on neural network systems including Generative Adversarial Networks (GANs) and transformer-based structures like Generative Pre-trained Transformer (GPT). Deep learning models generate new outputs through training on extensive datasets which teaches them to predict the next elements in sequences and improve their results through repeated refinements.

How Generative AI Differs from Traditional AI

Traditional AI systems are primarily designed for analyzing data, recognizing patterns, and making predictions. For example, a traditional AI model might be used for spam detection in emails, fraud detection in financial transactions, or diagnosing medical conditions based on historical data. These systems rely on predefined rules or supervised learning, where they are trained to classify or predict outcomes based on labeled datasets.

On the other hand, generative AI takes it a step further by not just analyzing data but also creating new data. Instead of merely identifying whether an email is spam, a generative AI model could write a convincing email based on a given prompt. Similarly, rather than just recognizing an image, generative AI can create entirely new images that never existed before. This creative capability distinguishes generative AI from traditional AI and expands its range of applications significantly.

Why Generative AI Matters

Generative AI technology is transforming industry landscapes while expanding AI capabilities. These factors demonstrate why generative AI has such a significant impact:

- **Enhancing Creativity and Innovation** – Generative AI can assist artists, writers, designers, and musicians by generating ideas, drafts, or even finished works, sparking creativity and streamlining the creative process.
- **Automating Content Generation** – Businesses can leverage generative AI to produce marketing materials, news articles, product descriptions, and even video content, significantly reducing time and effort.
- **Personalizing User Experiences** – AI-generated content can be tailored to individual preferences, such as personalized chat interactions, custom recommendations, and adaptive learning materials in education.
- **Advancing Scientific Research** – Generative AI is being used in drug discovery, material science, and other research fields to generate novel hypotheses, chemical compounds, and solutions to complex problems.
- **Closing the Divide Between People and Machines** – With the ability to generate human-like text, images, and speech, generative AI improves human-computer interaction, making AI-powered assistants and tools more intuitive and effective.

Generative AI enhances traditional AI by not only analyzing and interpreting data but also generating realistic and innovative outputs. This shift from descriptive and predictive analytics to creative and productive applications marks a major leap in the AI field.

Summary

While AI might seem like a complex topic, at its heart it's all about creating smart systems that can help humans in a variety of ways. While having a general sense of how AI functions is certainly beneficial, it's not necessary to grasp every intricate detail to make effective use of its tools. Thankfully, many AI applications come with intuitive interfaces and built-in automation that conceal the underlying complexity. This enables individuals and businesses to handle tasks like data analysis, customer engagement, and content creation—even without fully understanding every technical aspect. The more you learn about AI, the better equipped you'll be to harness its benefits and make informed decisions about its influence on your life and the world around you. In the next chapter, we'll explore specific examples of how AI is already transforming various industries and making everyday tasks easier than ever before.

2

AI IN EVERYDAY LIFE

AI has quietly woven itself into nearly every aspect of modern life, shaping how we communicate, work, shop, and even take care of our health. From the smartphone in your pocket to the smart devices in your home, AI is driving convenience, efficiency, and personalization. It drives virtual assistants that predict user requirements, fitness apps that track health metrics, and systems that optimize daily routines. Beyond personal use, AI is also reshaping entire industries, revolutionizing fields like healthcare, finance, and retail. This chapter highlights how AI is already integrated into our lives and how it will likely become even more common, often in ways we may not immediately recognize.

AI IN YOUR POCKET: SMARTPHONE APPS THAT USE AI

It's fair to say that smartphones have become an extension of daily life, handling tasks that once required multiple devices and hours of effort. It's rare to find someone without one, and for good reason—these AI-powered tools do far more than make calls and send texts. They organize schedules, provide real-time navigation, enhance photos, track health metrics, and even streamline shopping experiences by recommending products, comparing prices, and handling mobile payments—all from the palm of your hand. From the moment you wake up to the second you set your alarm at night, AI is working behind the scenes. Even while you sleep, apps driven by AI analyze sleep patterns, provide insights on rest quality, and offer recommendations to improve your overall well-being.

One of the most obvious ways AI enhances smartphone use is through virtual assistants like Google Assistant and Siri. These intelligent companions go beyond setting alarms and sending texts—they recognize your voice, answer questions, provide recommendations, and even learn your preferences to anticipate your needs. Whether you need directions, reminders, or weather updates, your virtual assistant acts as a personal manager, keeping you organized with just a simple voice command.

Photography has also been transformed by AI-powered apps, making capturing and editing images effortless. With automatic adjustments for lighting, color balance, and object removal, your photos can always look their best thanks to AI. Advanced features such as background blurring, facial recognition, and scene enhancement turn amateur snapshots into professional-quality images, all without the need for extensive editing skills.

AI is also breaking down communication barriers through real-time translation apps that enable conversations across languages. Whether traveling abroad or speaking with someone who doesn't share your native language, translators provide instant, accurate translations of spoken or written words. Then there's speech-to-text features that allow for quick note-taking and hands-free messaging, making everyday interactions smoother and more accessible.

If you own a smartphone, you are already using AI every day —whether you realize it or not. As the technology continues to evolve, smartphones will only become more capable, further integrating into routine tasks and reshaping how we work, communicate, and interact with the world.

SMART HOMES: MAKING YOUR HOME WORK FOR YOU

Even our homes are becoming smarter, transforming from static living spaces into intelligent environments that anticipate needs and respond to daily routines. However, while smartphones have become almost universal, smart home technology is still in the early stages of widespread adoption. But as AI-driven devices become more affordable and accessible, more households are beginning to embrace these innovations. Smart homes are no longer a luxury or a distant concept—they are steadily becoming the standard for modern living. With AI-powered technology, homes can now adjust lighting, regulate temperature, secure entry points, and even clean themselves, all while learning and adapting to personal preferences.

At the core of this transformation are AI-powered systems designed to optimize such functions seamlessly. Smart thermostats like Google Nest and Ecobee learn daily routines and temperature preferences, automatically adjusting settings to ensure comfort while reducing energy consumption. Intelligent lighting systems like Philips Hue and LIFX function as responsive technologies that adjust to natural lighting conditions and user presence to ensure adequate illumination while saving electricity. These advancements make homes more energy-efficient, lowering utility costs without sacrificing convenience.

Security is another area where AI is making a significant impact. Modern smart home security systems go beyond simple surveillance—they analyze footage in real time, distinguishing between routine activity and potential threats. AI-powered cameras like the Ring Video Doorbell and Arlo Pro can differentiate between a passing car, a pet, or an unknown visitor, sending alerts only when necessary. Smart locks such as August Smart Lock and Schlage Encode add another layer of protection, allowing homeowners to lock and unlock doors remotely, ensuring security even when they are away.

Back inside the home, robotic vacuums like the iRobot Roomba and Ecovacs Deebot navigate around furniture, keeping floors clean without manual effort. Also driven by AI, voice-controlled entertainment systems, like Amazon Echo and Google Nest Hub, provide hands-free access to music, movies, and smart TV functions with simple verbal commands. Smart appliances such as Samsung Family Hub refrigerators, which track groceries and suggest recipes, and June smart ovens, which adjust cooking times based on AI food recognition, simplify household management and streamline daily routines.

AI IN PERSONAL FINANCE: BUDGETING AND INVESTMENT TOOLS

Managing personal finances can be overwhelming, but AI-powered tools are making it easier than ever to track spending, set budgets, and invest wisely. These intelligent applications act as virtual financial advisors, offering real-time insights, automating money management, and providing personalized recommendations. Whether you're looking to cut costs, make smarter investments, or get a clearer understanding of your finances, AI-powered tools can help make managing money simpler.

For everyday budgeting, AI-powered apps like Mint, YNAB (You Need a Budget), and PocketGuard automatically categorize transactions, track spending patterns, and offer tailored financial advice. These apps provide a clear breakdown of expenses, helping users identify areas to cut costs and improve savings. By analyzing past spending habits, AI can even predict future expenses, offering proactive suggestions to keep you on track financially. Instead of manually entering expenses, these tools streamline budgeting, making financial management effortless and more intuitive.

AI also plays a major role in investing. Betterment, Wealthfront, and Ellevest are automated investment platforms that utilize AI algorithms to understand market movements and automatically adjust investment portfolios according to each client's risk preferences and financial objectives. Unlike traditional financial advisors, these robo-advisors provide data-driven insights without high fees, making investment strategies more accessible to everyday users. Additionally, stock analysis platforms such as Zacks Investment Research and Tickeron offer real-time market insights, analyze historical data, and predict trends to help investors make informed decisions quickly and confidently.

Security is obviously a top priority when dealing with financial data, which is why AI-driven finance tools incorporate advanced security measures to protect sensitive information. For example, encryption ensures that personal and banking data remain private, while two-factor authentication (2FA) provides additional protection by requiring users to complete a second verification step after entering their password. Many platforms also use AI-powered fraud detection, which monitors transactions for unusual activity and alerts users of potential threats in real time. These protections help ensure that financial data remains secure while allowing users to manage their money with peace of mind.

RETAIL AND E-COMMERCE: PERSONALIZING SHOPPING EXPERIENCES

Online shopping has become a daily convenience for millions of people, with e-commerce platforms offering everything from groceries to luxury goods at the tap of a button. Whether you're browsing for new running shoes, ordering office supplies, or searching for the perfect gift, AI is working in the background to enhance your shopping experience.

One of AI's most noticeable contributions to e-commerce is its ability to personalize shopping experiences. Recommendation engines analyze browsing history, past purchases, and even time spent on specific products to suggest items tailored to individual preferences. This technology, used by platforms like Amazon, eBay, and Shopify, acts as a virtual personal shopper, curating selections that align with a customer's unique style and interests. By predicting what shoppers might want next, AI is actively increasing convenience, improving customer satisfaction, and driving brand loyalty.

Beyond recommendations, chatbots have revolutionized customer service in online retail. Powered by AI, these digital assistants provide real-time support, answering inquiries, suggesting products, and assisting with checkout. Unlike human customer service representatives, AI chatbots operate 24/7, offering immediate help without wait times. They can process multiple requests at once, handle returns, and even learn from past interactions to improve their responses.

AI is also used in inventory management, helping retailers maintain the right stock levels without overordering or running out of popular products. AI-powered forecasting tools use historical sales data combined with seasonal patterns and external factors such as weather conditions to help businesses achieve accurate demand predictions. Take retailers like Walmart and Zara as examples, both of which use AI-driven inventory systems to monitor stock in real time, automatically triggering restocks when needed. This minimizes waste, reduces storage costs, and ensures that customers find the products they want when they need them.

Consumer insights are another area where AI is making a significant impact. Sentiment analysis tools scan product reviews, social media conversations, and customer feedback to gauge public opinion on products and services. Retailers use this data to refine marketing strategies, improve product offerings, and respond to customer needs more effectively. AI-driven marketing platforms, such as those used by Nike and Target, analyze consumer behavior to deliver personalized advertisements, promotions, and email campaigns that resonate with specific customer segments.

AI-POWERED EXERCISE AND FITNESS: TRACKERS AND SMART WELLNESS TOOLS

AI has become an essential part of personal health and fitness, offering smarter ways to monitor well-being and optimize workouts. From tracking daily activity to analyzing sleep patterns and even detecting potential health issues, AI-powered health tools have transformed how people engage with their fitness goals. Devices and apps equipped with AI don't just collect data—they provide personalized insights, helping users make informed decisions about their health with minimal effort.

AI-powered wearables like the Apple Watch, Fitbit Sense, and WHOOP go beyond merely counting steps. These devices monitor heart rate, blood oxygen levels, sleep cycles, and stress levels, using AI to analyze trends and offer actionable recommendations. For example, Fitbit's Sleep Score evaluates sleep quality based on heart rate variability and movement, while Apple's ECG feature can detect irregular heart rhythms, potentially alerting users to early signs of heart conditions. These health tracking features allow users to understand how their bodies respond to different activities, helping them make meaningful lifestyle adjustments.

Beyond tracking, AI is revolutionizing fitness coaching with personalized workout plans that adapt to progress over time. Apps like Freeletics, Nike Training Club, and Future use AI to generate custom workout routines based on fitness levels, goals, and past performance. Tempo Move and Peloton Guide take it even further, using AI-powered motion tracking to assess form and provide real-time feedback during workouts. These tools keep users motivated and ensure they exercise safely and effectively, offering the experience of a personal trainer without the high costs.

Incorporating AI into health and fitness isn't just about convenience—it's about empowering people with knowledge and motivation. These tools bridge the gap between data collection and meaningful action, turning everyday habits into smarter choices for long-term well-being.

AI IN HEALTHCARE: REVOLUTIONIZING DIAGNOSIS AND TREATMENT

AI is revolutionizing the healthcare industry. From detecting diseases earlier to optimizing treatment plans and even discovering new drugs, the technology is playing a major role in many aspects of patient care, benefiting both doctors and patients.

In radiology, AI-powered systems analyze X-rays, MRIs, and CT scans with remarkable precision, identifying abnormalities that might be overlooked by the human eye. Deep learning algorithms can detect signs of cancer, fractures, and other conditions faster and with greater accuracy than traditional methods. For example, AI-assisted screening tools can assess mammograms for early signs of breast cancer, providing radiologists with a second opinion that enhances their ability to make informed decisions. Additionally, predictive AI models analyze patient history and medical records to forecast potential health risks, giving doctors a proactive approach to disease prevention and treatment planning.

Once a diagnosis is confirmed, AI helps healthcare professionals develop individualized treatment plans. Medical platforms analyze patient data to propose ideal medication dosages and modify treatments for chronic conditions while creating customized interventions from individual health profiles. For conditions like diabetes, AI-powered systems can monitor glucose levels in real time and suggest insulin adjustments, helping patients maintain better control over their health. Similarly, AI algorithms assist in oncology by analyzing genetic markers to determine the most effective cancer treatments for individual patients, reducing trial-

and-error in medication selection and improving treatment outcomes.

The pharmaceutical industry is also benefiting, with AI revolutionizing drug discovery by accelerating research and development processes. AI models analyze vast chemical and biological datasets to predict which drug compounds are most likely to succeed in treating diseases. Instead of taking years to identify viable drug candidates, the technology can simulate interactions between drugs and biological systems, significantly reducing the time needed for early-stage research. It is also enhancing clinical trials by predicting which patients are most likely to respond to a new drug, optimizing trial designs, and increasing the likelihood of successful outcomes.

Despite its transformative potential, AI in healthcare comes with limitations and risks that necessitate careful oversight. While AI can process vast amounts of medical data, it lacks human intuition, ethical reasoning, and contextual understanding, which are crucial in complex medical cases. Errors in AI predictions, if left unchecked, can have severe consequences for patient safety. To mitigate these risks, human oversight remains essential—healthcare professionals must validate AI-generated insights, interpret recommendations in the context of each patient's unique circumstances, and ensure ethical standards are upheld.

AI IN EDUCATION: PERSONALIZED LEARNING

AI is transforming education as we know it. Instead of a one-size-fits-all approach, platforms driven by AI work to adapt to each student's strengths, weaknesses, and learning pace. By doing so, they are able to provide customized instruction that help maximize understanding. For example, if a student excels in reading but struggles in math, the AI system adjusts its lessons, dedicating more time to math practice while continuing to reinforce reading skills. This individualized approach keeps students engaged at a pace that suits them, reducing frustration and enhancing comprehension.

AI is also enhancing engagement through immersive learning experiences. Virtual reality (VR) and augmented reality (AR), powered by AI, bring subjects to life in ways traditional teaching methods cannot. Students are now able to explore ancient civilizations, conduct virtual science experiments, or interact with mathematical theories in a visual and interactive way. These experiences make learning more dynamic and memorable, catering to different learning styles.

Teachers also benefit from AI, as it reduces time-consuming administrative tasks and enhances both the learning and teaching experience. Automating grading, attendance tracking, and lesson planning helps educators save valuable time and maintain consistency. By minimizing paperwork and optimizing workflow, AI enables teachers to dedicate more time to engaging with students.

Despite its benefits, AI in education presents some notable challenges. Students without reliable access to technology may miss out on AI-driven learning opportunities, and underfunded schools may struggle to provide AI-powered tools, widening the gap between those with and without access to cutting-edge technology. Additionally, high-quality AI-powered learning platforms, VR tools, and data-driven analytics systems often require significant investment, forcing schools to balance the benefits of AI with budget constraints to ensure that technology adoption does not come at the expense of other essential educational resources.

Another issue is the over-reliance on technology. While AI can personalize learning, it cannot replace the human connection between teachers and students. Education involves emotional intelligence, critical thinking, and mentorship—qualities that AI cannot fully replicate. Excessive dependence on AI-based learning tools may limit students' chances to nurture interpersonal skills and participate in valuable conversations with teachers and fellow students.

Summary

Hopefully, you can now see just how widespread AI already is, shaping everything from daily routines to major industries. The examples in this chapter are only supposed to provide a glimpse of AI's vast influence, as its reach extends far beyond what can be covered here. As it continues to evolve, AI will become even more integrated into our lives in ways we are only beginning to imagine. With this growing presence, you may be wondering how to harness its power for your own benefit. Whether you want to boost productivity, automate tasks, or explore AI-driven creativity, there are many beginner-friendly tools available. In the next chapter, we'll explore some of the most accessible AI tools in more detail, how they work, and practical ways to start using them.

3

AI TOOLS FOR BEGINNERS

AI stands out by transforming complex processes into simple tasks while making advanced technology accessible to everyone. Designed for beginners, this chapter will provide guidance on selecting AI tools that enhance both personal and professional productivity. Whether you want to automate routine work, generate content, or simply experiment with AI's capabilities, we'll explore some of the most accessible and powerful tools available today—along with practical guidance on how to start using them right away.

GETTING STARTED WITH AI: CHOOSING THE RIGHT TOOLS

With so many tools available, choosing the right ones can feel overwhelming. When evaluating your options, consider both personal and professional tasks that could benefit from automation or AI assistance. Start by identifying repetitive or time-consuming activities—like scheduling, content creation, or data organization—that an AI tool could simplify. To avoid feeling overloaded, begin with one or two basic tools that fit your needs and then explore additional ones as your confidence grows. Clarifying your priorities will help you select tools that provide real value rather than unnecessary complexity.

When evaluating AI tools for work, remember to consider company policies and workplace guidelines. The tools you can use may depend on your job role or employer, as not all AI solutions are suitable for every work environment. For example, some may be restricted due to data security concerns, software compatibility, or compliance regulations. So with that in mind, before integrating AI into your workflow, it's essential that you ensure any tool is approved by your employer and aligns with company security protocols and its technological infrastructure.

When comparing the many AI tools available, make sure to read user reviews and get expert opinions to gauge their effectiveness and reliability. Pay close attention to features, functionalities, and how well they integrate with the tools you already use. For instance, if you're considering an AI scheduling assistant, ensure it syncs with your existing calendar apps.

Usability is another key factor to consider. Opt for tools with intuitive interfaces that don't require extensive training or technical expertise, allowing you to start using them effectively right away. Additionally, try to prioritize tools that offer robust customer support and tutorials, as having access to helpful resources and responsive assistance can make a significant difference, especially when you're new to AI.

The rest of this chapter will present a selection of AI tools that are especially suitable for beginners. These have been chosen for their user-friendliness, accessibility, and ability to deliver significant benefits with minimal setup. If you're unsure where to start, these recommendations will give you a solid foundation. In later chapters, we will explore additional AI tools designed to maximize productivity and creativity. Whether aiming to improve your personal life or optimize your professional tasks, these solutions will provide a practical starting point.

GRAMMARLY: ENHANCE YOUR WRITING WITH AI ASSISTANCE

Grammarly is a user-friendly AI tool that anyone can start using right away. With a quick setup, it effortlessly enhances daily writing tasks. As an accessible introduction to AI-powered productivity, Grammarly is a great starting point for beginners looking to improve their communication.

Struggling to perfect an email, blog post, or report? Maybe you're refining a social media update or crafting a standout cover letter. That's where Grammarly helps. This AI-powered tool enhances your writing—whether you're drafting a message, polishing a presentation, or updating your LinkedIn profile. Acting as a smart writing assistant, Grammarly catches errors and improves clarity, ensuring your words are polished and professional. It's like having a personal editor, offering real-time suggestions to help you communicate with confidence.

Unlike the basic spell check in Microsoft Word, which primarily focuses on identifying misspelled words and simple grammatical errors, Grammarly goes a step further by analyzing sentence structure, tone, clarity, and engagement. It provides real-time suggestions to improve readability, eliminate wordiness, and ensure your writing aligns with your intended audience. Whether you're aiming for a formal, persuasive, or conversational tone, Grammarly adapts to your writing style and offers context-aware recommendations.

Where Grammarly's versatility really shines is through its ability to integrate with various platforms, ensuring that your writing remains polished across different applications. For those who rely on Microsoft Office, it connects directly with Word and Outlook, bringing its editing features straight into your workflow. This allows you to receive real-time suggestions while working on documents and emails, eliminating the need to switch between programs.

Instructions to Get Started with Grammarly

1. **Visit the Grammarly Website** – Start by navigating to Grammarly's website (Grammarly.com) where you can find detailed information about the tool and its features.
2. **Download the Browser Extension** – From the website, download the Grammarly browser extension. This extension is compatible with most major browsers and integrates easily with your web activities.
3. **Install the Extension** – Follow the instructions provided to add the downloaded extension to your preferred browser. This step is usually straightforward and involves clicking an “Add” or “Install” button.

4. **Create an Account** – Provide the necessary basic details to sign up.
5. **Configure Your Preferences** – During the setup, you can configure your writing preferences. Whether you're aiming for a formal tone or a more conversational approach, setting these preferences helps Grammarly tailor its suggestions to your unique voice.
6. **Choose Your Plan** – Decide between the free version and the premium subscription. The free version offers basic checks for grammar, spelling, and punctuation—ideal for casual writing. The premium version includes advanced features, including style and tone adjustments, plagiarism detection, and sophisticated suggestions for word choice and sentence structure. This is suitable for more polished and professional writing needs.
7. **Start Writing** – With Grammarly installed and set up, it will work in the background as you write, whether you're composing emails, preparing reports, or posting on social media. It provides real-time feedback and suggestions without overshadowing your personal style.

VIRTUAL ASSISTANTS: MEET SIRI, GOOGLE ASSISTANT, AND ALEXA

As we touched on earlier, virtual assistants are another simple way to start implementing AI in your daily life. A big advantage of virtual assistants is their ease of use. They require no technical skills—if you can talk or type, you can interact with them. They are designed to be intuitive and user-friendly, making them an excellent entry point for those new to AI. Additionally, they are powerful time-saving tools. Whether it's setting reminders, scheduling meetings, or managing to-do lists, virtual assistants handle routine tasks efficiently, allowing users to focus on more important work.

Beyond productivity, virtual assistants offer the convenience of hands-free operation. Voice commands enable users to interact with their devices while cooking, exercising, parenting, working, or driving. They also learn from user behavior, gradually providing more personalized recommendations and responses over time. Another major benefit is their easy integration with everyday tools. From email and calendars to smart home devices, virtual assistants work across multiple platforms to streamline daily activities.

The widespread usage of virtual assistants means numerous resources exist to assist you in maximizing their potential. Whether it's online tutorials, community forums, or tech support, finding guidance is easy. In fact, you likely already know someone who regularly uses a virtual assistant and can provide tips or answer questions based on their experience.

If you have an iPhone, iPad, or Android phone, or own a smart speaker, you already have access to a powerful AI assistant. Below, we'll go over how to use Siri (Apple devices), Google Assistant (Android and Google devices), and Alexa (Amazon smart devices) to boost your productivity and simplify your routine.

Using Siri on an iPhone or iPad

Siri comes pre-installed on iPhones and iPads which allows users to start using it by either a voice command or by pressing a button. You can activate Siri by going to "Settings > Siri & Search," where you'll find the option to enable "Hey Siri" for hands-free voice activation. Alternatively, you can activate Siri by pressing and holding the home button on older iPhones or the side button on newer models.

Siri is a convenient tool for managing tasks, setting reminders, and executing quick actions without physically touching your device. You can use it to send messages, control smart home gadgets, or check the weather. Need a quick unit conversion while cooking? Siri delivers instant answers. On the move and need to send a text? Siri allows you to do it completely hands-free.

Here are a few examples of how you can use Siri:

- **Set Reminders and Alarms**: "Hey Siri, remind me to call Mom at 6 PM."
- **Send a Message**: "Hey Siri, send a text to John saying 'I'll be there in 10 minutes.'"
- **Get Directions**: "Hey Siri, give me directions to the nearest coffee shop."
- **Control Smart Devices**: "Hey Siri, turn off the bedroom lights."
- **Check Weather Updates**: "Hey Siri, do I need an umbrella today?"

Using Google Assistant on Android Phones and Google Devices

For those with Android smartphones or Google smart devices, Google Assistant is a powerful AI tool that can help you with various tasks. You can activate Google Assistant by saying "Hey Google" or "OK Google" or by pressing and holding the power button on some Android devices. Users who do not have the Google Assistant app on their device can download it from the Google Play Store.

Google Assistant is particularly useful for managing schedules, searching for information, and controlling Google-compatible smart home devices. If you're driving and need directions, Google Assistant can guide you without needing to touch your phone. If you're preparing for a meeting, it can read your schedule aloud.

Here are some ways to get the most out of Google Assistant:

- **Manage Your Schedule**: "Hey Google, what's on my calendar today?"
- **Send Messages Hands-Free**: "Hey Google, send a WhatsApp message to Lisa saying 'See you at lunch.'"
- **Translate Languages Instantly**: "Hey Google, how do you say 'thank you' in French?"
- **Control Smart Home Devices**: "Hey Google, turn on the living room lights."
- **Get Real-Time Traffic Updates**: "Hey Google, how long will it take to get to the airport?"
- **Play Music or Podcasts**: "Hey Google, play my 'Focus' playlist on Spotify."

Using Alexa with Amazon Devices

Unlike Siri and Google Assistant, Alexa is primarily used with Amazon Echo smart speakers and other Alexa-enabled devices. To access Alexa, you'll need a compatible device such as an Amazon Echo, Echo Dot, or Echo Show. Once you've set up your device using the Amazon Alexa app, you can activate Alexa simply by saying "Alexa," followed by your request.

Alexa is particularly useful for managing shopping lists, controlling smart home devices, and playing music. If you want to create a grocery list hands-free, Alexa can store your items for you. If you need to dim the lights or adjust your thermostat, Alexa can handle it with a voice command. It can also help you wind down at the end of the day by playing ambient sounds or guided meditations.

Here are a few ways to use Alexa effectively:

- **Create Shopping Lists**: "Alexa, add eggs, milk, and bread to my shopping list."
- **Control Home Automation**: "Alexa, dim the lights to 50%."
- **Get a Flash News Briefing**: "Alexa, give me the latest headlines."
- **Set a Timer While Cooking**: "Alexa, set a timer for 20 minutes."
- **Play Audiobooks**: "Alexa, read my book from Audible."

Which Virtual Assistant Should You Use?

Each virtual assistant—Siri, Google Assistant, and Alexa—has its own strengths, unique features, and limitations. While all three share core functions such as setting reminders, answering general knowledge questions, and controlling compatible smart devices, they each excel in different areas based on their ecosystems and primary use cases.

Siri is best suited for those who own multiple Apple devices, as it works best across iPhones, iPads, MacBooks, Apple Watches, and HomePods. Deeply embedded in Apple's ecosystem, Siri is ideal for users who rely on Apple services such as iMessage, FaceTime, Apple Music, and iCloud. It excels in device continuity, allowing users to send messages, make calls, and control settings with ease across Apple products. However, Siri has fewer third-party integrations than Google Assistant and Alexa, making it most effective within Apple's ecosystem.

Google Assistant stands out for its powerful search capabilities, making it particularly strong at answering complex questions with Google's vast knowledge base. It integrates well with Google services like Gmail, Calendar, Maps, and Google Home devices, allowing users to manage schedules, navigate efficiently, and get real-time search results. Google Assistant also supports natural language processing and contextual follow-ups, making conversations more fluid. Additionally, it offers extensive third-party integrations with smart home devices, entertainment platforms like Spotify and Netflix, productivity tools such as Slack and Trello, and popular services like Uber and WhatsApp, enhancing its versatility.

Alexa is a top choice for smart home control. It works with thousands of third-party devices and features, making it highly versatile. Primarily designed for Amazon Echo speakers and displays, Alexa lets users manage smart home gadgets, stream music, and shop on Amazon using voice commands. It also integrates with many third-party services like Ring, Nest, SmartThings, Spotify, Apple Music, Uber, Pandora, Audible, and Zoom. While Alexa's functionality is expansive, it's mostly designed for home use, not mobile integration. Although available on smartphones through the Alexa app, it isn't as effective as Siri or Google Assistant for mobile tasks.

Choose the virtual assistant that fits your needs and start using it today. Try out its features, explore its integrations, and see how it can make your life easier.

AI IN THE KITCHEN: MEAL PLANNING AND GROCERY SHOPPING MADE EASY

Grocery shopping, meal planning, and cooking are essential parts of most people's daily routine. Despite their importance, these tasks can often become time-consuming and tedious, especially amid our busy schedules. The good news is that AI meal planning apps are transforming these necessary activities into more efficient and manageable tasks.

Getting started with AI meal planning apps is generally straightforward. With just a few simple steps to set up your dietary preferences and restrictions, they tailor meal recommendations to fit your specific nutritional needs and culinary tastes. Whether you have specific dietary goals, food allergies, or personal taste preferences, these apps adjust to meet your requirements with minimal effort on your part. They also allow you to easily specify portion sizes, which is perfect for individual meals or family dinners, ensuring each dish is just right for your needs.

Once set up, the apps shine by automating the more cumbersome aspects of meal management, such as grocery shopping. They generate shopping lists from your selected meal plans, saving you the hassle of manual list-making and ensuring you never forget an ingredient again. These lists can be dynamically adjusted if you change your meal plan last minute, and many apps integrate directly with online grocery stores, enabling you to complete your shopping with a few clicks from anywhere.

AI meal planning apps go beyond convenience—they actively support healthier eating habits by monitoring nutritional intake and offering insights into your daily diet. By analyzing the nutritional content of each meal, these apps can recommend healthier ingredient alternatives when specific nutrients are lacking. This feature is particularly useful for individuals following strict dietary guidelines or aiming to enhance their overall well-being.

These tools are ideal for beginners looking to incorporate technology into their daily routines. By leveraging AI-powered solutions, you can simplify meal management, making it a more enjoyable and effortless part of your day.

Common AI Meal Planning Apps to Try

- **Eat This Much**: This app automatically generates meal plans based on your food preferences, nutritional goals, and budget. It can accommodate various diets like vegan, ketogenic, paleo, and more. The app also offers grocery lists and can send them directly to grocery delivery services.
- **Mealime**: Mealime supports healthy eating through easy-to-use personalized meal plans that address different dietary needs and food allergies. It provides detailed grocery lists and recipes for cooking in 30 minutes or less.
- **PlateJoy**: PlateJoy creates personalized meal plans based on a detailed quiz that covers your dietary preferences, health goals, time constraints, and more. It includes grocery lists that integrate with grocery delivery services and offers digital pantry tracking.

CHATGPT: YOUR AI-POWERED CONVERSATION PARTNER

By now, you've likely heard of ChatGPT, an advanced AI language model from OpenAI that's gaining popularity among both tech enthusiasts and everyday users. As part of the GPT-3.5 series, ChatGPT represents a major leap in generative AI, allowing machines to better understand and generate human-like text with remarkable accuracy. ChatGPT is powered by a system with 6.7 billion parameters, which help it understand and generate text naturally. These parameters act like guidelines or rules that allow the AI to recognize language patterns, sentence structures, and context. ChatGPT analyzes vast amounts of text data to understand how words and ideas connect. Its advanced processing methods help make its replies sound more conversational and less robotic.

Despite its advanced capabilities, ChatGPT is easy to integrate into everyday life. With its user-friendly interface, it's accessible to everyone—not just tech experts. It can be used for a wide range of tasks, including:

- **Writing and Editing** – Generate articles, blog posts, emails, resumes, and other content.
- **Customer Support** – Respond to inquiries, troubleshoot issues, and automate customer interactions.
- **Brainstorming and Creativity** – Provide ideas for projects, marketing strategies, storytelling, and more.
- **Learning and Research** – Explain complex topics, summarize information, and provide study assistance.
- **Coding Assistance** – Debug code, suggest improvements, and help with programming questions.

- **Language Translation** – Translate text between languages with impressive accuracy.
- **Task Automation and Productivity** – Set reminders, manage schedules, and offer workflow suggestions.
- **Casual Conversation and Entertainment** – Engage in friendly chat, play games, and provide recommendations.

To start using ChatGPT access the chat box located at the screen's bottom and begin typing in your message. After typing your prompt or query just press "Enter" or click "Send" to submit it. The AI will analyze your input and provide a response which gets displayed in the conversation window positioned above the chat box. The interactive format promotes a seamless dialogue which enables users to easily ask additional questions or adjust their prompts according to the responses given. Specific instructions for setting up and using ChatGPT will be given in the following chapter.

Summary

Exploring AI tools firsthand is the best way to see their potential. This chapter introduced some beginner-friendly tools, each offering practical benefits with minimal setup. To truly understand their impact, choose one that interests you and start experimenting with its features today. The next chapter will provide detailed instructions on using ChatGPT and crafting effective prompts to maximize its potential. Get ready to explore the full capabilities of this powerful AI tool and enhance your interactions with AI technology.

4

CHATGPT: A BEGINNER'S GUIDE

Prepare to embark on your journey with ChatGPT. This simple yet powerful tool is designed for people of all skill levels. Whether you are curious about AI, looking to optimize your workflow, or simply need assistance with daily decisions, ChatGPT is ready to help. It can support research, enhance writing, and act as a personal assistant to guide decision-making. In this chapter, we'll explore how to use ChatGPT effectively with practical examples and sample prompts to help you get started.

START USING CHATGPT TODAY

Setting up ChatGPT is a simple process. To get started, visit the ChatGPT website (chat.openai.com). Here, you'll find an option to sign up or log in. New users can create an account, which involves providing an email address, creating a password, and possibly verifying the email address through a link sent to your inbox. Once your account is set up, you can start using ChatGPT immediately.

ChatGPT is available in two versions: a free version and a subscription-based option called ChatGPT Plus. The free version is a great starting point for beginners, offering plenty of functionality for everyday tasks like answering questions, generating content ideas, and exploring new topics.

However, for those who need enhanced performance and additional benefits, ChatGPT Plus provides several advantages for a monthly fee. These include priority access to new features and updates, faster response times, and higher usage limits during peak hours, making it a valuable option for frequent users. If you're unsure whether you need the paid version, start with the free plan and upgrade if needed.

Crafting Effective Prompts: Tips and Tricks for Beginners

In the realm of ChatGPT, a prompt serves as the starting point for interaction. It's like a question or statement you feed into the AI to guide its response. Think of it as giving directions; the clearer your directions, the better the AI can navigate. A well-crafted prompt can transform a conversation with ChatGPT from mundane to insightful. When we talk about prompts, we're referring to the input you provide, which could be as simple as asking, "What's the weather like today?" or as complex as requesting a detailed summary and critical analysis of a multi-page scientific article. The beauty of ChatGPT lies in its ability to understand and respond to these prompts, making it a versatile tool for various applications.

The clarity and specificity of your prompts are crucial. Imagine asking someone, "Tell me about history." The response would be broad and possibly overwhelming. Instead, if you narrowed it down to "Tell me about the history of ancient Egypt," you'd receive a more focused and informative answer. ChatGPT operates in a similar way. Vague prompts result in scattered responses, while specific ones lead to precise and relevant answers.

To maximize the effectiveness of your prompts, consider incorporating open-ended questions and relevant context. Open-ended questions encourage more detailed responses, allowing ChatGPT to provide richer information. For instance, rather than asking "Is Paris a nice city?" you could ask, "What are some interesting cultural activities to explore in Paris?" Adding context helps ChatGPT tailor its response to your needs. If you're inquiring about a historical event, stating the event and the aspect you're interested in—like its impact on modern society—will yield a more useful answer. Including background information ensures that the AI understands your query's nuances, leading to more accurate responses.

Let's now explore some examples of well-crafted prompts. Suppose you're looking for creative ideas for a social media campaign. A prompt like "Generate engaging content ideas for a new fitness app launch" gives ChatGPT clear direction, leading to relevant suggestions. Or, if you need a summary of complex information, you might say, "Summarize the key points of a recent study on workplace productivity trends." These prompts are specific and provide context, guiding the AI to deliver responses that meet your expectations.

10 Tips for Writing Effective ChatGPT Prompts

Use these tips to help you craft effective prompts that maximize the utility and accuracy of responses from ChatGPT:

1. **Be Specific** – Clearly define what you need from the response. The more specific your question, the more targeted and useful ChatGPT's answer will be.
2. **Provide Context** – Include relevant background information in your prompt. This helps ChatGPT understand the framework within which it should generate a response.
3. **Use Clear and Concise Language** – Avoid vague terms and be concise. This reduces the chance of misinterpretation and helps ensure that you receive a direct answer.
4. **Specify the Desired Detail Level** – Indicate whether you want a brief overview or a detailed explanation.

This guides the model in tailoring the complexity and length of its response.

5. **Sequential Questioning** – If you have a complex topic, break it down into a series of questions to be asked one at a time. This sequential questioning can lead to more comprehensive and understandable information.
6. **Include Examples** – If applicable, provide examples to illustrate the type of information or solution you are seeking. This is especially useful for creative tasks.
7. **Request Summaries or Bullet Points for Clarity** – If you're looking for clarity and brevity, ask for responses in the form of summaries or bullet points.
8. **Use Correct Terms and Names** – Ensure you use the correct terminology and proper names related to your question. This helps in generating accurate and relevant responses.
9. **Limitations Acknowledgment** – Recognize and consider the limitations of the AI. For complex or nuanced queries, factor in that you might need to refine the prompt or seek expert human advice.
10. **Feedback Loop** – If the initial response doesn't fully meet your needs, use it as a base to refine your question further, providing feedback or additional information as needed.

LEVERAGING CHATGPT FOR RESEARCH, INFORMATION, AND LEARNING

In an era of constant information flow, finding, organizing, and understanding knowledge efficiently is more important than ever. ChatGPT functions as a valuable resource in both research and education by enabling rapid access to data while simplifying complex subjects and enhancing learning. Whether you're conducting research as a professional, working on an assignment as a student, or simply eager to learn more, ChatGPT can make the process more efficient and engaging.

We've all experienced the challenge of sifting through endless sources of information for a project or research. Thankfully, ChatGPT can make this less overwhelming by summarizing lengthy articles, breaking down difficult concepts, and offering structured outlines for papers or reports. For example, if you're researching the impact of remote work on employee productivity, ChatGPT can provide a concise summary of key findings, suggest reputable sources to explore, and even help outline your report. However, while AI is a great starting point for research, users must confirm data accuracy using trustworthy and verified sources. AI-generated content should complement—not replace—traditional research methods.

ChatGPT also acts as a versatile learning tool, making education more accessible and personalized. Students can use it to get explanations on challenging subjects, create study guides, and generate practice questions. Whether you're unraveling the mysteries of quantum physics, decoding an ancient manuscript, or learning a new language, ChatGPT can offer step-by-step explanations that cater to different learning styles. Professionals and lifelong learners can benefit as well, using ChatGPT to stay updated on industry trends, summarize complex reports, or explore new skills. Instead of passively consuming information, AI allows for interactive learning by adapting responses based on user input.

Despite its advantages, using AI for research and education requires a thoughtful approach. Because ChatGPT doesn't have real-time access to the internet and relies on pre-existing knowledge, some information may be outdated or incomplete. It's important to cross-check findings, refine search queries for better accuracy, and use ChatGPT as a supplement rather than a sole source of information. Additionally, asking AI for sources or citations can help direct users toward more authoritative references.

The true power of AI in research and education lies in its ability to save time by streamlining information gathering, simplifying complex topics, and enhancing interactive learning experiences. By using ChatGPT strategically—whether to outline reports, practice new skills, or generate discussion topics—users can make learning and research more efficient, allowing them to focus on deeper understanding rather than tedious tasks.

Sample Prompts for Research and Learning

- "Provide a step-by-step solution to the algebra equation: 5x - 3 = 2x + 9."
- "Generate six discussion questions about the Industrial Revolution for a history class."
- "Translate this sentence into Spanish and explain the grammar rules: 'She is going to the store.'"
- "Explain the significance of the Renaissance in European history in a paragraph."
- "Describe Einstein's theory of relativity to high school students using straightforward language and familiar examples."
- "List five academic sources that examine the impact of remote learning on student performance and engagement in higher education."

STREAMLINING YOUR WRITING TASKS WITH CHATGPT

Writing is a crucial skill in both personal and professional life, whether you're drafting emails, blog posts, reports, or creative pieces. However, finding the right words is often challenging. ChatGPT can be a tremendous help by generating ideas, refining drafts, and enhancing clarity. One of its biggest advantages is assisting with everyday writing tasks like emails and reports. Crafting professional, well-structured emails can be time-consuming, but ChatGPT ensures they are clear, polite, and to the point—whether responding to a colleague, following up with a client, or making a persuasive request. Similarly, for reports and business documents, it helps organize information, summarize key points, and improve readability, ensuring polished and professional content.

For marketers and content creators, ChatGPT is a valuable tool for drafting blog posts, social media content, and other marketing materials. If you're struggling to come up with engaging topics, ChatGPT can even generate ideas based on your audience and industry. It can also help with structuring articles, writing compelling headlines, and optimizing content for readability. For social media posts, ChatGPT can suggest engaging captions, hashtags, and ideas tailored to different platforms.

Beyond business and content creation, ChatGPT is also a powerful resource for creative writing. Whether you're working on a novel or screenplay, it can help you brainstorm plot ideas, develop characters, and refine dialogue. If you hit a creative block, ChatGPT is on hand to suggest alternative storylines or fresh perspectives to keep your project moving forward. Additionally, the technology allows writers to experiment with different tones and styles, making it easier to adapt their writing for various genres and audiences.

While ChatGPT is a powerful tool, it's important to use it thoughtfully. Maintaining originality and authenticity in your writing is crucial, whether you're drafting professional content, marketing materials, or a creative project. AI can enhance your work by providing suggestions, improving structure, and eliminating writer's block, but it should not replace your unique voice and critical thinking. Additionally, ensuring that AI-generated content aligns with ethical writing practices—such as avoiding plagiarism and respecting intellectual property—should always be a priority.

Examples of ChatGPT Prompts for Writing Tasks

- "Write a polite email requesting a meeting with a potential client about our new product launch."
- "Compose a professional follow-up email to thank the interviewer for their time, express enthusiasm for the role, and reiterate your qualifications."
- "Help me write a formal resignation letter with a two-week notice."
- "Write a catchy Instagram caption for a new coffee shop opening, including relevant hashtags."
- "Generate three different Instagram posts promoting an upcoming webinar on digital marketing."
- "Summarize this 10-page research report into a one-paragraph executive summary."
- "Write a dialogue exchange between a detective and a suspect in a mystery novel."

- "Rewrite this paragraph to make it clearer and more engaging: [insert text]."
- "Change the tone of this email from formal to friendly: [insert email]."

USING CHATGPT FOR PERSONAL ASSISTANCE AND DECISION-MAKING

Beyond work, education, and writing tasks, ChatGPT can act as a personal assistant, helping users stay organized, optimize their time, and simplify everyday tasks. Whether you're looking for entertainment recommendations, wellness advice, travel planning, or financial guidance, ChatGPT is here to help.

One of the easiest ways to use the platform in daily life is for personalized entertainment recommendations. For example, if you're searching for a new book, movie, or TV show, ChatGPT can provide suggestions based on your past favorites and genre preferences. By describing what you enjoy—whether it's fast-paced thrillers, lighthearted comedies, or historical fiction—it can generate lists of titles that align with your tastes. While AI can offer a solid starting point, entertainment preferences are of course highly personal, therefore reading reviews and watching trailers before committing to a selection is still a good practice.

ChatGPT can also assist with fitness, diet, and wellness guidance, offering exercise routines, meal planning ideas, and lifestyle tips based on specific goals. Whether you're looking for home workouts, healthy recipes, or stress-relief techniques, ChatGPT can generate helpful suggestions tailored to your needs. However, it's important to keep in mind that AI-generated health advice should never replace professional medical guidance. Nutrition, exercise, and wellness plans should be cross-checked with a certified trainer, registered dietitian, or doctor to ensure they are safe and suitable for your individual needs.

For those who enjoy traveling, ChatGPT can help with trip planning and itinerary creation. From suggesting destinations to outlining daily activities, it can offer travel advice based on your budget, interests, and timeframe. You can ask for recommendations on must-see landmarks, local dining options, and hidden gems to explore. However, AI-generated travel information should always be verified for accuracy, as details like business hours, pricing, and availability may change frequently. Checking official tourism websites and recent traveler reviews is a great way of ensuring that plans remain up-to-date and reliable.

Another way ChatGPT can enhance personal decision-making is by offering basic financial planning and budgeting tips. Whether you want to create a monthly budget, explore investment options, or understand credit management, ChatGPT can simplify financial concepts into easy-to-understand advice. It can suggest methods for saving money, tracking expenses, and managing debt. However, for more complex financial matters like investment strategies, tax planning, or major financial decisions, it's always recommended to consult a certified financial advisor before taking action.

Sample Prompts for Personal Assistance and Decision-Making

- "Recommend a mystery novel similar to 'Gone Girl' with a psychological twist."
- "Suggest five comedy TV shows with lighthearted humor and quick episodes."
- "Create a weekly workout plan for a beginner looking to improve endurance."
- "What are some healthy meal ideas for a vegetarian diet with high protein intake?"
- "Plan a three-day itinerary for New York City, including must-see attractions and restaurants."
- "Recommend budget-friendly travel destinations for a solo traveler in Europe."
- "Explain the 50/30/20 budgeting rule and how I can apply it to my monthly expenses."
- "What are some strategies for saving money on everyday expenses?"

MAXIMIZING CHATGPT'S POTENTIAL

We've already detailed some beginner uses of ChatGPT, but the possibilities are truly endless. For those looking to dive deeper, advanced applications of this technology can significantly transform the way you work and create.

For instance, ChatGPT can assist in programming by debugging code or suggesting optimizations. It can also simulate conversational models for training customer service bots, providing a safe and controlled environment to refine responses before they reach actual users. In the realm of research, ChatGPT has the ability to help synthesize vast amounts of data into comprehensible summaries, aiding in the discovery of patterns and findings that might otherwise be missed.

A key technique for maximizing ChatGPT's potential is mastering advanced prompt writing. Crafting well-structured, detailed prompts can dramatically improve the accuracy and depth of responses. Instead of asking simple questions, users can provide context, specify tone and format, and even define step-by-step instructions. For example, rather than asking, "How can I improve my writing?" a more advanced prompt would be: "Analyze this paragraph for clarity and engagement, then suggest three improvements based on readability, conciseness, and tone." By incorporating such techniques, you can guide ChatGPT to deliver more precise and relevant outputs.

For complex tasks, chaining prompts can be highly effective. This involves breaking down a request into multiple, sequential prompts that build on previous responses. For instance, if you're writing an article, you can start with a brainstorming prompt, then refine your ideas, outline key points, and finally request detailed paragraph development. This iterative approach helps produce high-quality, well-structured content.

Advanced Prompting Techniques to Consider

1. **Advanced Contextual Prompts** – Provide specific background or contextual information about your query. For example, if you're working on a marketing campaign include details such as the target audience, brand tone, and key objectives. Supplying this context helps ChatGPT tailor its responses to your specific scenario.
2. **Role-Based Instructions** – Instruct ChatGPT to assume a particular role or perspective. Phrases like "Act as an expert data analyst" or "Respond as a professional resume editor" guide the model to generate specialized responses, helping you get precisely what you need.
3. **Step-by-Step Reasoning** – Encourage ChatGPT to detail the reasoning behind its answers or to break down complex problems into smaller parts. This technique clarifies the logic chain and can reveal insights you might otherwise miss.
4. **Specify Output Format** – For clearer responses, define the format you need. Whether it's a bulleted list, numbered steps, executive summary, formal email, or comparison table, specifying structure

ensures clarity and usability. You can also request bold text for emphasis, like key points in a summary or section headings in a guide. A well-formatted prompt helps ChatGPT deliver structured, easy-to-read content tailored to your needs.

5. **Ask ChatGPT** – If you're unsure how to phrase your prompt, ask ChatGPT for guidance. Start with a rough idea and refine it by requesting suggestions or examples. For instance, you can say, "Help me write a prompt for a detailed business proposal" or "How can I improve this prompt to get a more structured response?" ChatGPT can suggest refinements, add constraints, or clarify wording to help you craft the most effective prompt for your needs.

Maximizing ChatGPT's potential requires understanding its limitations as well as its capabilities. As we mentioned earlier, the technology does lack real-time internet access, which means it may generate outdated or inaccurate information. It can also struggle with nuanced context, sometimes producing responses that lack depth or miss the intended meaning. Additionally, because ChatGPT learns from existing data, it may reflect biases present in that data, leading to unintentional bias in its responses. It does not possess true reasoning or independent thought—it simply predicts likely responses based on input. Over-relying on AI for writing or decision-making can also limit critical thinking and creativity, making it essential to use ChatGPT as a tool rather than a replacement for human judgment.

Summary

The best way to fully grasp ChatGPT's capabilities is simply to start using it for a variety of tasks. Begin with straightforward queries or projects, and as you gain familiarity with the tool—especially how to craft more precise prompts—you'll be able to unlock a whole new world of advanced features and integrations. However, as AI tools like ChatGPT become more widely used, it's crucial to recognize their limitations and ethical implications. In the next chapter, we'll explore the ethical considerations of AI and the responsibility that comes with its growing role in our lives.

5

THE ETHICS OF AI

As AI takes on decisions once made by humans, it is essential to consider not just its potential but also its limitations and ethical challenges. This chapter will explore key ethical considerations, including transparency, accountability, and privacy, to ensure the responsible use and development of AI. We will also examine its impact on jobs and the economy, addressing concerns about automation, workforce displacement, and emerging opportunities in an AI-driven world. Additionally, common misconceptions about AI will be debunked, as we seek to clarify myths that often fuel fear and misunderstanding. While we may not have all the answers, asking the right questions and understanding these challenges allows us to guide AI's evolution as a force for progress rather than harm.

ETHICAL FOUNDATIONS: TRANSPARENCY, ACCOUNTABILITY, AND PRIVACY

Imagine receiving a job offer purely based on an algorithm's decision or commuting in a self-driving car making split-second choices that could affect your safety. Picture a doctor relying on an AI-powered system to diagnose a critical illness or a bank determining your loan eligibility based on machine-generated risk assessments. These scenarios aren't just futuristic—they're happening right now. But as AI takes on more responsibility in decision-making, critical questions arise: How can individuals trust these decisions, especially when the reasoning behind them is often opaque? And if something goes wrong—whether it's a misdiagnosis, an unfair rejection, or an accident—who is to blame? Furthermore, as AI systems process vast amounts of personal data to make these determinations, concerns about privacy and data security become more pressing. Who has access to this information, how is it being used, and what protections exist to prevent misuse? These questions of transparency, accountability, and privacy form the foundation of the most critical ethical challenges AI must address.

Transparency: Understanding AI's Decision-Making

Transparency is one of the foremost ethical challenges of AI. Many AI models function as "black boxes," meaning their decision-making processes are difficult, if not impossible, to interpret. This is especially concerning in fields such as finance, law enforcement, and healthcare where AI-driven decisions can have life-altering consequences.

For individuals, a lack of transparency can result in a sense of helplessness when facing AI decisions that impact their lives. For example, if an AI system determines eligibility for a college application or decides who qualifies for a government benefit, the person affected has no way of understanding or disputing the decision. This lack of clarity can breed frustration, diminish trust, and potentially cause harm.

To improve transparency, researchers and policymakers are advocating for explainable AI, which seeks to make AI decision-making more interpretable. Explainability initiatives are focusing on developing models that provide clear, step-by-step reasoning for their outputs. In addition, regulations such as the General Data Protection Regulation (GDPR) require AI systems to offer explanations for significant automated decisions. Organizations deploying AI are also being encouraged to adopt open-source AI models and ensure that their algorithms undergo external audits to verify fairness and reliability.

Accountability: Who is Responsible When AI Goes Wrong?

Another crucial question in AI ethics is accountability—who is responsible when AI makes a mistake? If a self-driving car causes an accident or an AI-based hiring system unfairly rejects a candidate, determining blame can be complex.

Unlike traditional decision-making, which involves a clear human actor, AI systems distribute responsibility across developers, companies, regulators, and users.

For individuals, AI-driven errors can have profound effects on their lives, influencing opportunities, financial stability, and personal well-being. The complexity of AI accountability makes it challenging to seek recourse when errors occur, leaving people vulnerable to decisions that may not be easily contested or corrected.

The good news is that efforts are already well underway to address these accountability challenges. One approach is the implementation of AI auditing frameworks, which assess how decisions are made and identify biases in datasets. Governments and regulatory bodies are also developing legislation to ensure that AI developers follow ethical guidelines.

Another proposed solution is the concept of "human-in-the-loop" AI, where human oversight is incorporated into critical decision-making processes. This approach ensures that AI-generated recommendations are reviewed before final decisions are made, reducing the risk of errors and providing a clearer chain of accountability. Furthermore, organizations are increasingly required to maintain detailed documentation of their AI models, ensuring that biases and potential risks are addressed before deployment.

Despite these advancements, challenges remain. The pace of AI development often outstrips the creation of effective regulations, leaving gaps in oversight. Moreover, international collaboration is necessary to establish standardized accountability measures, as AI systems operate across global markets.

Ultimately, accountability in AI requires a multi-faceted approach involving technological advancements, legal frameworks, and ethical considerations. By prioritizing transparency, oversight, and human involvement, society can mitigate the risks associated with AI errors and ensure that responsibility is properly assigned when mistakes occur. Achieving this, however, will require collaborative efforts from policymakers, technologists, industry leaders, and the public to create a balanced and responsible AI ecosystem.

Privacy: Protecting User Data in an AI-Driven World

AI systems thrive on data—personal, financial, medical, and behavioral information that helps them make predictions and automate decisions. However, this reliance on data raises serious privacy concerns. Many users are unaware of the extent to which their information is collected, shared, or used to influence decisions about them. Facial recognition technology, targeted advertising, and AI-driven surveillance have all sparked debates about the ethical boundaries of data collection.

To address these privacy issues, several data protection laws have been implemented globally. We've mentioned GDPR in Europe, which sets a high standard for data privacy and security. It gives individuals more control over their personal data, requiring organizations to obtain explicit consent before collecting or processing it. The GDPR also mandates transparency, allowing you to know what data is collected and how it's used. Likewise, in the United States, the California Consumer Privacy Act (CCPA) empowers consumers to know about and control the personal information businesses collect. These regulations are crucial in protecting your rights and ensuring that your data is handled responsibly.

Alongside legal frameworks, privacy-enhancing technologies play a significant role in safeguarding your information. Encryption is a key method, ensuring that data is securely stored and transmitted, making it accessible only to authorized users. Data anonymization is another technique where identifiable details are removed, making it difficult to trace data back to you. Differential privacy techniques enable data analysis while safeguarding individual privacy by introducing "noise" into datasets, making it difficult to identify specific individuals. These technologies help create a safer digital environment, allowing you to benefit from AI without compromising your privacy.

As an individual, there are also proactive steps you can take to protect your privacy when using AI tools. A great way to start is by reviewing and managing app permissions on your devices. This means checking which apps have access to your data and adjusting settings to limit unnecessary access. For instance, if a weather app requests access to your contacts, consider whether this is truly necessary for its function. Additionally, opting for privacy-focused AI applications can provide an extra layer of security. These are designed with user privacy in mind, often offering enhanced control over data collection and usage.

Privacy Checklist

To enhance your privacy when using AI apps, streamline your approach with this practical checklist:

- **Review Privacy Settings** – Open each app's settings, navigate to "Privacy" or "Security," and adjust settings to limit data sharing, and disable unnecessary data collection like location tracking.
- **Understand Data Collection** – Before downloading any new app, find and read its privacy policy. Scroll to the sections labeled "Data Collection" and "Third-Party Sharing"and note what data is collected and shared. Use browser extensions like "Terms of Service; Didn't Read" to get a summarized version. If the policy seems too permissive, consider seeking alternatives that respect privacy more.
- **Limit Permissions** – For each app, go to your device's settings, select "Apps," find the app, and tap

"Permissions." Only enable permissions that are essential for the app's functionality.
- **Use Two-Factor Authentication (2FA)** – Enable 2FA on apps and services where available to bolster security.
- **Stay Informed** – Regularly update yourself on new updates and changes to privacy settings and policies. Subscribe to newsletters from trusted sources like the Electronic Frontier Foundation (EFF) or Cybersecurity and Infrastructure Security Agency (CISA). Set up Google Alerts for terms like "privacy updates" or "data security."

THE INFLUENCE OF AI ON JOBS AND THE ECONOMY

It's no secret that the rise of AI is reshaping the global job market and economy at an unprecedented pace. While AI-driven automation enhances efficiency and reduces costs, it is also transforming traditional employment structures. AI systems now perform numerous routine and repetitive tasks formerly done by humans particularly within the manufacturing, retail, and customer service sectors. To maintain their competitiveness workers are needing to adopt to changing roles and acquire new skills.

However, it's important to note that AI is not just eliminating jobs—it is also creating new opportunities. The growing demand for AI development, data science, and technology management has opened up new career paths that did not exist a decade ago. At a growing rate, companies are seeking professionals who can design, implement, and maintain AI-driven solutions. Additionally, AI is enabling new business models, automating tedious tasks, and allowing workers to focus on more strategic and creative endeavors.

The difficulty lies in ensuring a smooth transition for workers affected by automation. Without proper support, displaced employees may find themselves unable to compete in an AI-driven economy. To address this, governments, businesses, and educational institutions must collaborate to implement reskilling programs that equip workers with sufficient skills to thrive in the evolving job market. Initiatives such as job retraining, technical education, and career counseling can help workers transition into new roles and industries.

Proper management of AI systems can lead to groundbreaking innovation while boosting productivity levels and generating fresh economic benefits. While some industries will experience disruption, others will grow and evolve as AI continues to integrate into various sectors. Individuals and organizations must prepare for these changes to stay competitive in the environment of AI-driven business and technological landscapes.

Simple Ways to Adapt to AI in the Workplace

As AI continues to change the job market, it's natural to wonder how to stay relevant and adapt. The good news is that you don't need to be a tech expert or a programmer to keep up. There are some simple steps you can take to make the most of AI today and prepare yourself for the future.

One of the easiest ways to start is by learning more about AI in general. Reading this book is a great start! Additionally, there are many free and beginner-friendly online resources that explain how AI works in simple terms. Understanding the basics—such as how AI helps businesses, automates tasks, or improves decision-making—can give you a better sense of how it might affect your industry. You don't need to take complex coding courses; simply becoming familiar with the role AI is playing in different fields can help you stay informed.

It's also helpful to stay open to learning new skills. Many jobs will not disappear but instead evolve to include AI-powered tools. For example, office workers might use AI for organizing tasks, teachers might use it to personalize lessons, while marketers might analyze trends. Becoming comfortable with AI-powered tools, like chatbots or productivity software, can give you an advantage in your current job. Many of these tools are designed to be user-friendly, so you don't need a technical background to use them effectively.

Another great way to prepare for changes is to stay connected with others in your industry. Talking to coworkers, attending workshops, or joining online discussions about how AI is being used in your field can help you gain insights and ideas. Many people are in the same boat, figuring out how to adapt, so sharing experiences and learning together can make the process easier.

If you're thinking about switching careers or exploring new opportunities, consider looking into AI-related jobs that match your strengths. You don't have to become a programmer—a number of AI-related roles involve skills like problem-solving, communication, creativity, and organization. Exploring different options and seeing how AI fits into various industries can help you make informed career decisions.

The most important thing is to stay curious and flexible. AI is a tool that can help make work easier, and by taking small steps to learn and adapt, you can stay ahead without feeling overwhelmed. Instead of worrying about AI taking over, focus on how it can be used to support your goals and career growth.

DEBUNKING AI MYTHS: SEPARATING FACT FROM FICTION

AI is one of the most discussed and misunderstood technologies of our time. As the technology becomes increasingly embedded in daily life, myths and misconceptions about its capabilities and implications continue to spread. Let's now debunk nine of the most common AI myths and provide clarity on what AI truly is and isn't.

Myth 1: AI Thinks Like Humans

One of the most persistent misconceptions is that AI functions like the human brain. While AI can mimic certain cognitive tasks, it does not possess human-like reasoning, emotions, or consciousness. AI operates based on mathematical models and data-driven algorithms, rather than intuition or self-awareness. Even the most advanced AI models, such as ChatGPT, do not "think" independently; they process inputs and generate results based on patterns learned from vast datasets.

Myth 2: AI Will Replace Humans in All Jobs

The fear that AI will take over all jobs is widespread. While AI is automating many tasks—and even fully replacing certain roles in areas like data entry, basic customer service, and routine manufacturing—it is more likely to augment human roles rather than eliminate them entirely. AI excels at repetitive, data-driven tasks but struggles with complex problem-solving, creativity, and emotional intelligence—areas where human workers thrive. Instead of wiping out entire professions, it will reshape the job market, creating new opportunities while requiring workers to develop AI-related skills to stay relevant.

Myth 3: AI Is Infallible and Always Objective

AI is often perceived as an unbiased and flawless decision-maker. However, such systems are only as good as the data they are trained on. If an AI model is fed biased or incomplete data, it will produce biased or inaccurate results. AI is susceptible to errors, making human oversight crucial to ensuring fairness, accuracy, and ethical use. Organizations developing AI must prioritize transparency and accountability to mitigate unintended consequences.

Myth 4: AI Can Fully Understand and Replicate Human Emotions

AI does not truly "understand" emotions. While it can analyze text, speech, and facial expressions to detect sentiment, this does not equate to experiencing or feeling emotions like humans do. Emotional intelligence is a uniquely human trait, and AI should be considered as a tool to assist in emotional analysis rather than a substitute for human empathy.

Myth 5: AI Is a Recent Invention

Many assume AI is a recent phenomenon, but its conceptual roots date back to the mid-20th century. Early research laid the foundation for the technology we use today. Over the years, AI has gone through cycles of enthusiasm and stagnation—known as AI winters—before the rapid advancements of the past decade. This recent boom is not the result of a sudden invention but rather improvements in computational power, access to larger datasets, and more sophisticated algorithms.

Myth 6: AI Will Eventually Become Sentient and Take Over the World

A common trope in science fiction is the idea of AI becoming self-aware and overthrowing humanity. However, it is currently nowhere near achieving sentience. AI operates based on statistical correlations, predefined rules, and machine learning models without consciousness or self-preservation instincts. While ethical concerns about AI's misuse are valid, fears of an AI-driven apocalypse remain firmly in the realm of fiction.

Myth 7: AI Can Learn on Its Own Without Human Intervention

Some assume that AI can continuously learn and evolve on its own without human involvement. While models can improve through iterative learning, they require human engineers to provide new data, refine algorithms, and correct errors. AI systems are not able to set their own goals or develop new learning strategies without guidance from programmers.

Myth 8: AI Is Only for Large Tech Companies and Experts

Another misconception is that AI is only accessible to big corporations and highly skilled engineers. In reality, AI tools are becoming increasingly available to a wider audience. Many platforms offer user-friendly AI solutions for businesses and individuals, requiring little to no coding expertise. From AI-powered productivity tools to no-code machine learning platforms, the technology is more accessible than ever for small businesses, students, and everyday users.

Myth 9: AI Can Predict the Future with 100% Accuracy

While AI is highly effective at recognizing patterns and making predictions, it is not infallible. AI-driven predictions, such as those used in finance, healthcare, and weather forecasting, are based on probabilistic models that rely on historical data. Unforeseen variables and changing conditions can impact outcomes, meaning AI can never guarantee absolute certainty in its predictions. Simply put: human judgment remains essential in interpreting AI-driven insights.

Summary

AI is rapidly reshaping society, bringing both opportunities and challenges that require careful consideration. Dispelling myths, like those we have just covered, is critical for fostering a realistic and informed perspective on the technology. Rather than fearing AI or overestimating its capabilities, we should focus on leveraging its strengths while addressing its limitations responsibly. When used wisely AI is a game-changing tool that can enhance productivity, creativity, and decision-making across various fields. In the next chapter, we'll take a deeper look at how AI can be harnessed to boost productivity, streamline workflows, and empower individuals and businesses to work smarter, not harder.

6

ENHANCING PRODUCTIVITY WITH AI

When it comes to workplace efficiency and personal productivity, AI has truly become a transformative force. This chapter discusses how AI can be used to streamline routine tasks, support smarter decision-making, and foster collaboration. From optimizing inbox management and automating workflows to refining scheduling, AI-powered tools are on hand to help you save time and reduce mental load. However, the availability and implementation of AI tools can depend on your job, industry, and company rules. By gaining a clear understanding of AI's diverse applications, you can identify and utilize the right solutions to enhance your productivity and effectiveness.

STREAMLINING TASKS AND COMMUNICATION

In today's fast-paced work environment, AI is transforming how professionals manage communication, collaboration, and productivity. From streamlining email management to automating meeting notes and enhancing team coordination, tools powered by AI are reshaping office workflows. By integrating these intelligent solutions, organizations can optimize efficiency, reduce workload, and create a more seamless work experience.

Take the constant flood of emails for example, which can often be overwhelming. Thankfully, AI offers an effective solution with smart sorting algorithms. Tools like Shortwave and SaneBox analyze inboxes, prioritize important messages, and funnel newsletters or less urgent emails into separate folders. Some services, such as Superhuman, even provide AI-driven email composition suggestions based on individual writing styles. By managing the inbox and drafting replies, AI can declutter communication channels while safeguarding against overlooking vital information.

AI technology also enhances document collaboration, making teamwork more efficient. The likes of Google Docs and Microsoft 365 incorporate AI-powered add-ons to track changes, enforce version control, and suggest relevant content or edits in real time. These features minimize confusion over file versions while encouraging creative contributions by automating repetitive tasks. AI effectively becomes a behind-the-scenes assistant, allowing teams to focus on refining content and generating innovative ideas.

When it comes to internal team communication, AI-powered chatbots and virtual assistants resolve frequent bottlenecks. For example, Slack integrations can handle recurring HR queries on leave policies or benefits, while project management platforms like Asana and Trello use AI for automated task reminders. By taking care of routine inquiries and follow-ups, AI improves overall efficiency and prevents minor tasks from stalling important projects.

Note-taking tools are also revolutionizing how professionals capture and organize information. Applications such as Otter.ai, Notion AI, and Jamie use AI to summarize meeting notes, generate action items, and categorize information for easy retrieval. These tools can produce both concise notes and full transcriptions, making the process of taking meeting notes almost effortless. By eliminating the need to manually jot down key points, they help users avoid sifting through lengthy transcripts or disorganized notes, ensuring that key takeaways are highlighted and easily accessible for future reference. Whether used in meetings, brainstorming sessions, or research, AI-driven note-taking streamlines information management and enhances productivity.

As AI's role in office work continues to expand, these tools serve as collaborators rather than replacements. The automation of repetitive or time-consuming tasks provides more opportunities for you to engage in meaningful work, strengthen creative output, and maintain a healthier work-life balance. By embracing AI's extensive toolkit, offices can evolve into more efficient, innovative, and satisfying environments.

PROJECT MANAGEMENT

Managing projects with many people involved can often feel like a juggling act, with shifting deadlines, multiple stakeholders, and never-ending updates. Although it's not a cure-all, AI-powered project management software can help businesses of all sizes tackle many of these challenges. Platforms like Monday.com, Wrike, Trello, and Asana incorporate AI-enhanced features that prioritize the most critical tasks, helping your team stay focused. Automated notifications alert you to impending deadlines or sudden changes in scope, freeing you from the stress of constantly monitoring every detail. By analyzing project data to suggest optimal task allocations—based on team capacity, experience, and past performance—these tools ensure that all members are utilized effectively and efficiently.

Facilitating team collaboration also becomes more intuitive when AI steps in. Workload-balancing features in tools such as Asana and Wrike can look at each team member's current assignments and suggest reassignments where needed, preventing burnout and promoting maximum productivity. Predictive analytics forecast potential bottlenecks or delays, allowing teams to adjust their approach proactively. This level of insight transforms collaboration from reactive to strategic, empowering everyone to contribute while keeping projects on track and under budget.

AI goes further by enhancing decision-making through comprehensive data analysis that would otherwise take hours for humans to compile. Real-time dashboards in applications like Monday.com or Trello break down project metrics into clear visuals, allowing quick, evidence-based decisions. Risk assessments, generated by AI, highlight areas of concern while proposing solutions informed by historical data and predictive modeling. Such foresight gives managers the confidence to make calculated adjustments, ensuring decisions are guided by meaningful insights rather than just gut instinct.

Tracking progress and productivity also becomes more transparent thanks to AI-powered monitoring. For example, live updates display the status of tasks as they change, making it easier to refine plans on the fly. Comparative benchmarking against project milestones highlights whether the team is meeting—or exceeding—goals, and where improvements are needed. By presenting this information in accessible formats, AI fosters a sense of accountability and ownership, as each team member can see exactly how their contributions affect the bigger picture. In turn, leaders can identify top performers, offer targeted support, and maintain an engaged, motivated workforce.

To illustrate the impact of AI in project management, imagine a marketing firm launching a new product with multiple teams handling content creation, social media, and paid advertising under tight deadlines. Using an AI-driven project management tool, tasks are automatically assigned based on expertise and workload, while predictive analytics flag potential delays, such as a designer overloaded with revisions or a content approval stuck in review. Real-time dashboards provide instant visibility, allowing managers to redistribute tasks, adjust priorities, and ensure smooth collaboration. When AI detects an ad campaign outperforming projections, it reallocates the budget to maximize reach and engagement. By proactively managing resources and optimizing workflows, the firm meets its deadlines, improves team efficiency, and exceeds its campaign goals—demonstrating the tangible benefits of AI in project management.

SCHEDULING AND TIME MANAGEMENT

Managing your schedule can be surprisingly challenging in today's fast-paced environment, with an endless list of tasks, appointments, and reminders to keep track of. AI-driven scheduling tools aim to change that, offering a seamless way to coordinate your calendar and optimize how you spend your time. By automating key aspects of scheduling, these tools remove the stress of double bookings or overlooked meetings and give you back the mental bandwidth needed for more important duties.

To begin integrating AI scheduling into your routine, start by syncing these tools with your existing calendar platforms (e.g., Google Calendar or Outlook). This step ensures that updates made in one place instantly reflect across all your devices, allowing you to stay informed wherever you go. The result is a unified view of your commitments, reducing the confusion of managing multiple calendars at once. By merging everything into one system, it becomes much easier to see where you can fit in that crucial project work, networking call, or personal errand.

Once your calendars are synced, most AI scheduling apps automatically set up task reminders and alerts to help keep you on track. You can customize reminders for deadlines, meetings, or any other important events, and the apps will nudge you at precisely the right moment. These reminders adjust based on your interactions, ensuring that alerts remain relevant and timely without becoming disruptive. This proactive approach to managing your schedule helps you prepare for upcoming commitments and reduces the risk of last-minute rushes.

AI scheduling tools also offer insights into how you use your time, providing a clearer picture of your productivity. By analyzing data on your daily patterns, they can highlight periods where you are most effective or pinpoint tasks that consume more time than expected. You can use this information to align your most important responsibilities with your peak hours, ensuring you tackle your most challenging work when at your best. Identifying inefficiencies or bottlenecks through AI-generated reports empowers you to make meaningful changes, whether that means rescheduling certain tasks or delegating them altogether.

Incorporating AI into your time management strategies is not just about convenience; it can fundamentally reshape how you approach your day. These systems do more than send reminders and notifications. They help you balance your professional and personal commitments by dynamically adjusting to changes in your schedule and providing real-time updates that keep you organized. By removing the burden of constant calendar checks, AI scheduling tools free up cognitive space, enabling you to focus on big-picture thinking and more creative pursuits.

Several scheduling tools are available that are easy to use:

- **Reclaim.ai:** Uses AI to optimize your calendar by scheduling meetings and blocking time for focused tasks, adjusting dynamically to your routine.
- **Clockwise:** Optimizes your work schedule by rearranging meetings to create blocks of uninterrupted focus time.

- **x.ai:** Automates scheduling by handling back-and-forth communication, finding the best meeting times based on your preferences.
- **Cortana (Microsoft):** An AI assistant that manages calendars, schedules meetings, and sends reminders, integrating seamlessly with Outlook.

AUTOMATING REPETITIVE TASKS

Each day a significant amount of time is consumed by repetitive tasks that demand precision but offer little in the way of creative challenge. Data entry, for instance, involves transferring information into databases or spreadsheets—a routine that is critical to accuracy yet does not necessarily require human oversight. Another example is the cyclical process of report generation, which entails collecting, sorting, and formatting data to produce standardized documents. These tasks are ideal for AI automation, allowing you to save time and energy for more strategic responsibilities.

Robotic Process Automation (RPA) is a powerful approach to automating these types of structured, rule-based activities. Software from providers like UiPath, Automation Anywhere, and Blue Prism can replicate human actions by logging into applications, entering data, and performing calculations. Imagine a bot that updates your customer database each evening, using information extracted from incoming emails and forms. Such a setup eliminates human error while running tirelessly, ensuring that your data stays up to date without constant oversight. Similarly, data-scraping platforms such as Octoparse or Apify can collect and organize large volumes of web-based information, turning chaotic input into structured datasets ready for analysis.

In the area of customer service, AI chatbots now handle a growing share of routine inquiries. Platforms like Intercom or Dialogflow enable the creation of chatbots that address common questions—such as order statuses or return policies—24 hours a day, seven days a week. These bots continuously learn from user interactions, refining their answers to become increasingly accurate and contextually relevant. By automating repetitive customer support tasks, businesses can reduce operational costs, improve response times, and allow humans to focus on complex or high-value interactions.

AI can also integrate smoothly with existing workflows to streamline multi-step processes. Trigger-based automations in Customer Relationship Management (CRM) systems like Salesforce or HubSpot can initiate follow-up actions, such as sending welcome emails when new contacts are created. AI-driven document processing tools, like ABBYY or DocuSign Intelligent Insights, automatically sort and extract information from files, then route the data to the right destination. This synergy cuts down on manual intervention, bolsters consistency, and accelerates project timelines, leaving more room for strategic planning and innovation.

To ensure they remain effective, monitoring the performance of automated processes is vital. Tracking metrics like error rates and processing times can reveal where tweaks are needed, while feedback loops allow automated systems to learn from their own performance data. Over time, these refinements adapt the system to the evolving demands of your business, keeping your automation workflows current and relevant.

PERSONAL AND FAMILY LIFE

Saving time and increasing efficiency are crucial not only in the workplace but also in the hustle and bustle of daily life. Whether it's coordinating family schedules, handling household chores, or planning a vacation, streamlining tasks can make a big difference. By applying time-saving strategies across different areas of life, you'll create more time for loved ones—or even just for yourself.

AI-powered to-do list apps, like Todoist and Motion, are available which act as digital organizers. These tools use AI to analyze your habits and routines, learning which tasks are most important or time-sensitive. As a result, they can suggest the optimal order in which to tackle your tasks, ensuring that you're focusing on what's most urgent or requires the most energy. Additionally, these apps send reminders at precisely the right moments, helping you stay on track without the need for constant manual input. Unlike traditional to-do lists, which simply display tasks without offering any real-time guidance, these AI-driven apps adapt to your evolving needs. They adjust as your schedule changes, automatically rescheduling tasks, prioritizing based on deadlines, or even suggesting when to delegate or break tasks down into smaller steps. This dynamic approach ensures that nothing slips through the cracks, allowing you to manage your day with greater efficiency and less stress.

Family communication can be made simpler with AI-powered assistants like Amazon Alexa or Google Nest Hub, which we've already explored in more detail earlier in the book. These devices can help manage reminders for important tasks, such as picking up kids from practice, taking medications, or setting up appointments. By syncing with calendars and smart devices, these assistants help ensure nothing is forgotten. If you need to remind your child about completing their homework or making sure everyone remembers to take out the trash, you can easily set up voice-activated reminders.

FamiSafe is a family safety app that leverages AI to help parents monitor and manage their children's digital lives. It offers features designed to improve family time management and ensure safety, including screen time control, location tracking, and activity monitoring. Using AI, FamiSafe can analyze usage patterns and send alerts if children engage in inappropriate or risky behavior online, helping parents stay informed. Additionally, it allows parents to set time limits for apps, track real-time location, and even create geo-fences to receive alerts when children enter or leave specific areas. This AI-driven approach saves time by automating monitoring tasks and reduces stress by keeping parents informed and in control of their children's safety.

AI tools can also help families plan vacations or manage daily travel logistics. For instance, AI-powered apps like Google Travel and Kayak can find the best flights, hotel deals, and activity suggestions, while tracking your family's preferences. These tools not only save time but also reduce the stress of planning a trip, ensuring that all family members have a memorable vacation without the hassle of manual research. When it comes to everyday travel, the Waze GPS system uses AI to provide real-time traffic updates, suggest faster routes, and even predict the best times to leave based on your typical commute patterns, helping you avoid traffic and save time. Google Maps also leverages AI to analyze traffic flow, road conditions, and historical data, offering optimal routes and suggesting alternative paths when disruptions occur.

Summary

In this chapter, we explored how AI can boost efficiency in both professional and personal spheres. From automating repetitive tasks to streamlining communication and organizing schedules, AI tools can dramatically improve productivity and free up valuable time. The key is to explore and test different options until you find the tools that best suit your needs. As we move into the next chapter, we will explore how AI can fuel creative endeavors, bridging technology and artistry to inspire new forms of innovation. This shift will show how AI not only enhances efficiency but can also become a powerful ally in unleashing creativity.

7

CREATIVE USES OF AI

Fueled by imagination, emotion, and experience, creativity has long been considered a uniquely human trait. But AI is reshaping that notion, emerging not just as a tool but as a collaborator in artistic expression. From painting and music to writing and design, AI is unlocking new creative possibilities. This is allowing both professionals and hobbyists to push the boundaries of what's possible. Whether it's generating stunning visuals, composing symphonies, assisting with storytelling, or refining graphic designs, AI-powered tools are making the creative process more accessible, efficient, and innovative. In this chapter, we'll explore how AI is transforming the arts, enhancing human creativity, and even challenging our understanding of originality and authorship.

VISUAL ARTS

Imagine standing in an art gallery, captivated by a painting that seems to pulse with life, its colors subtly shifting as you move. This isn't just a static work of art—it's an interactive experience brought to life by AI. By redefining the boundaries of creativity, AI offers artists innovative tools and possibilities that once belonged to the realm of science fiction. Whether you're an artist eager to explore new mediums or an admirer of visual art, AI challenges you to rethink what's possible in the creative world.

AI art generation tools are at the forefront of this transformation, opening doors to creativity that were previously locked. Take DeepArt.io, for instance—a platform that transforms ordinary photos into extraordinary artworks by applying the styles of famous paintings. Imagine uploading a snapshot of your favorite sunset and seeing it reimagined in the style of Van Gogh's "Starry Night," with swirling skies and vibrant colors. This process, known as style transfer, allows anyone to become an artist, creating unique pieces without needing traditional art skills. DeepArt.io's user-friendly interface means that all you need is an internet connection and a photo to get started, making it accessible to everyone, regardless of their technical background.

Another remarkable tool is DALL-E, developed by OpenAI. This neural network creates images from text descriptions, turning words into visual art. Picture typing "a two-headed flamingo standing in a field of lavender" and watching as DALL-E brings this whimsical scene to life with stunning detail. DALL-E's capabilities extend beyond mere image creation; it can manipulate the attributes of objects and combine unrelated concepts, offering an endless playground for imagination. This tool exemplifies how AI can synthesize creativity and technology, pushing the limits of what we conceive as art. It's a testament to how AI can serve as a collaborator, helping artists materialize visions that might otherwise remain confined to the mind's eye.

Beyond creating new art forms, AI also enhances traditional artistic techniques. Imagine an AI tool that suggests color palettes based on the composition and mood of your piece, guiding you toward harmonious and visually striking combinations. These AI-driven suggestions can spark creativity, offering new perspectives and possibilities. Moreover, AI can automate image enhancement and correction, adjusting lighting, sharpness, and contrast to bring out the best in your artwork. This frees artists from the technical hassle, allowing them to focus on their creative expression. By integrating AI into the artistic process, artists can achieve greater precision and efficiency, making the creative journey as fulfilling as the final result.

The potential of AI extends into the realm of interactive art installations, where it creates dynamic experiences that engage audiences in real time. Imagine walking into a room where the art responds to your presence, changing colors or shapes as you move. Motion-detecting installations use sensors to trigger visual changes, creating a conversation between the viewer and the artwork. AI-driven visual projections can go a step further, responding to audience interaction with evolving patterns or narratives, making each visit a unique experience. These installations transform art from a passive viewing experience into an active engagement, blurring the lines between creator and observer. By embedding AI into these installations, artists can craft immersive environments that captivate and inspire.

However, the rise of AI-generated art brings with it important ethical and copyright considerations. As the technology becomes a co-creator, questions about authorship and intellectual property arise. Who owns the rights to artwork created in collaboration with AI? How do we ensure that AI-generated pieces are original and not mere replicas or derivatives? These debates challenge traditional notions of creativity and ownership, prompting artists and legal experts alike to navigate new ethical landscapes. Ensuring originality and avoiding plagiarism become crucial as AI tools can easily replicate styles and techniques. We will discuss these ethical and copyright considerations in more detail later in the chapter.

MUSIC GENERATION

Picture yourself sitting at a piano, fingers poised, ready to create a melody that captures your mood. Now imagine having an AI collaborator by your side, ready to suggest harmonies, rhythms, and even entire compositions. AI music composition software has opened new avenues for musicians and enthusiasts alike, providing tools that transform the way music is created. Software like Amper Music stands out as a leading choice for generating music tracks. With its vast library of sounds and intuitive interface, Amper allows users to compose original pieces with ease. Whether you're crafting a soundtrack for your latest video or just exploring musical ideas, Amper offers a user-friendly experience that brings your musical visions to life. It doesn't matter if you're a seasoned musician or a complete beginner, Amper's AI capabilities make music composition accessible to all.

Similarly, AIVA, or Artificial Intelligence Virtual Artist, specializes in composing orchestral pieces. This tool is particularly adept at creating symphonies that rival compositions by human composers. AIVA's algorithms analyze a vast repertoire of classical music to generate pieces that are both complex and emotionally resonant. This allows musicians to experiment with orchestral arrangements without needing a full orchestra at their disposal. Whether you're composing for a film score or an independent project, AIVA provides the tools to create richly layered compositions that evoke the grandeur of a live performance.

The beauty of AI in music lies in its ability to explore diverse genres effortlessly. With this technology at your fingertips, you can venture into electronic beats, crafting catchy rhythms that pulse with energy. AI tools are also on hand to suggest bass lines, synth patterns, and even vocal effects, helping you build tracks that resonate on the dance floor. On the other end of the spectrum, AI can assist in creating classical symphonies, offering insights into structure, melody, and instrumentation. By combining traditional and contemporary styles, AI allows musicians to explore new musical landscapes, blending genres in innovative ways.

Beyond composing new pieces, the technology plays a significant role in enhancing existing compositions. Think of it as a digital sound engineer, capable of refining your music to perfection. AI-assisted remixing can transform a simple track into a complex arrangement, adding depth and variety. In audio production, AI analyzes frequencies, adjusting levels for clarity and balance. It also suggests harmonization and orchestration, helping you experiment with new musical textures. These enhancements not only improve sound quality but also unlock creative possibilities, encouraging exploration beyond conventional approaches.

Finally, let's talk about how AI is redefining the live music experience. Musicians are incorporating AI into their sets, allowing for real-time improvisation that adds an element of surprise and spontaneity. AI can generate visuals that sync with the music, creating a captivating experience for audiences. Imagine a live band accompanied by AI-generated visuals that change with the beat, enhancing the emotional impact of the performance. The use of AI brings a new dimension to live music, where technology and artistry converge to create unforgettable experiences.

CREATIVE WRITING

Imagine staring at a blank computer screen and unable to find the right words. It's a challenge many writers face. But now, imagine having an AI writing assistant by your side, ready to spark creativity when inspiration runs dry. Tools like Sudowrite and Wordtune have emerged as invaluable partners in the creative process. Sudowrite is particularly adept at brainstorming ideas, generating plot twists, and suggesting fresh angles, helping writers escape the confines of the dreaded writer's block. By feeding it a few lines or ideas, you receive suggestions that can take your story in exciting new directions. Wordtune, on the other hand, focuses on refining language and style, offering alternatives that enhance clarity and elevate your writing without overshadowing your unique voice. These AI tools do not replace the writer but serve as catalysts for creativity, offering a new way to engage with the written word.

The collaborative potential of AI in writing is a game-changer for authors. Think of it as a co-author, one that never tires, bringing fresh perspectives to the table. Imagine starting with a basic premise and having the AI suggest potential plot points, allowing you to explore different story arcs with ease. In character development, it can assist by generating detailed backgrounds and traits, ensuring your characters are as vivid as they are complex. Additionally, AI input in dialogue creation can help craft conversations that feel natural and engaging, adding depth to interactions between characters. This collaboration between human creativity and AI ingenuity results in stories that are rich and multifaceted, where ideas evolve through a blend of human and machine.

Exploring narrative variations becomes a breeze with AI at your disposal. Writers often ponder the "what if" scenarios—alternate endings, different paths taken by characters, or even shifts in narrative voice. AI provides a platform to test these variations without the laborious task of rewriting entire sections. You can experiment with different narrative perspectives, trying out first-person intimacy or third-person omniscience, and see how these shifts affect the story's impact. This flexibility not only enriches the writing process but also enhances the reader's experience by providing diverse narrative possibilities, inviting them to engage with the story in multiple ways.

However, as with any tool, the use of AI in writing brings with it questions of creative authenticity and ethics. There's a delicate balance between leveraging AI's capabilities and maintaining your voice and style. It's essential to ensure that while AI can suggest and assist, the personal voice remains predominant. With this in mind, writers must navigate the fine line between inspiration and imitation, ensuring that their work is not only distinctive but also respectful of intellectual property.

GRAPHIC DESIGN

Graphic design has always been about visual storytelling, a blend of artistry and communication. Today, AI tools are reshaping this landscape, making design more accessible and efficient. Platforms like Canva and Adobe Sensei offer features that optimize workflows and amplify creativity. Canva's AI-driven layout suggestions help create visually appealing designs by optimizing balance, color, and symmetry. Adobe Sensei focuses on intelligent image editing, using machine learning to automate tasks like retouching, cropping, and enhancing.

AI is even on hand to facilitate creative workflow automation. Imagine needing to resize an image for various social media platforms—traditionally, a time-consuming process. AI can automate this, adjusting dimensions and maintaining quality across formats. Batch processing further simplifies your work, allowing you to apply changes to multiple design elements simultaneously. By freeing up precious time, these capabilities allow you to concentrate on innovation and creativity.

In logo design, AI-powered tools like Looka and Tailor Brands generate unique, professional-quality logos based on user preferences. By analyzing industry trends, typography, and color psychology, AI suggests refined design options that align with brand identity. While designers can further customize these AI-generated concepts, the technology accelerates the brainstorming process, offering fresh ideas that might not have been considered.

Beyond automation, AI fosters innovation by pushing creative boundaries. By iterating through multiple design variations, it helps identify the most effective visual solutions. These tools inspire new ideas and unconventional approaches, encouraging designers to step beyond traditional methods and explore new creative possibilities.

NAVIGATING LEGAL AND ETHICAL CHALLENGES IN AI-GENERATED CREATIVITY

As we touched on earlier, with AI becoming an increasingly integral part of creative expression, legal and ethical questions surrounding ownership, copyright, and intellectual property are gaining prominence. The rise of AI-generated content introduces complexities that challenge traditional legal frameworks, prompting discussions on who owns AI-assisted works, how originality is defined, and what legal protections are available.

Ownership and Copyright of AI-Generated Works

One of the most pressing legal concerns surrounding AI-generated content is determining ownership. Traditional copyright law grants authorship to human creators, but when AI plays a significant role in generating a piece of artwork, music, or text, the question arises: Who holds the rights?

In many jurisdictions, copyright law does not currently recognize AI as an author. Instead, ownership typically falls to the human who programmed the AI, provided the AI's contribution is considered a tool rather than an independent creator. However, this distinction becomes blurred when AI generates complex works with minimal human input. Courts and lawmakers are actively discussing whether AI-generated works qualify for copyright protection and, if granted, who holds ownership.

The Role of Human Input

The level of human involvement in the creative process significantly impacts copyright claims. If an artist uses AI as a tool—such as employing AI to enhance an image or generate text suggestions—then the final work is more likely to be considered the artist's intellectual property. However, if an AI model independently creates a painting or composes a piece of music without substantial human intervention, ownership becomes more ambiguous.

For example, the U.S. Copyright Office has ruled that AI-generated works, without significant human creativity, cannot be copyrighted. This means that businesses or individuals using AI-generated content may face difficulties in protecting their work from unauthorized use. Consequently, creatives leveraging AI tools must ensure they provide meaningful input into the creative process to retain copyright protections.

Plagiarism and Derivative Works

Another legal concern is the potential for AI-generated content to infringe upon existing copyrighted works. AI models are often trained on datasets which include copyrighted materials. If an AI generates a piece of art or musical composition that closely resembles an existing copyrighted piece, it could lead to accusations of plagiarism or copyright infringement.

AI-generated content challenges traditional definitions of derivative works, particularly in cases where it modifies or transforms existing material. For example, if an AI model is trained on the style of a particular artist and then generates a similar piece, does it constitute an unauthorized derivative work? Artists and content creators must be cautious when using AI-generated elements to avoid potential legal disputes. While legal frameworks are still evolving, some companies are implementing guidelines to ensure that AI-generated content does not directly replicate copyrighted materials.

Ethical and Commercial Considerations

Beyond legal concerns, ethical considerations also play a role in AI-assisted creativity. Transparency and attribution are crucial—should AI-generated works be clearly labeled to distinguish them from human-created content? Some argue that consumers and audiences have a right to know whether an artwork, song, or written piece was AI-generated.

From a commercial standpoint, businesses and individuals using AI-generated content should be aware of licensing agreements and intellectual property policies of AI tools. Some AI platforms retain partial ownership or require licensing fees for commercial use, which could impact creators' ability to profit from their work. Before integrating AI-generated content into commercial projects, it is essential to review the terms of use and potential restrictions imposed by AI service providers.

The Future of AI and Intellectual Property Law

As AI continues to reshape creative industries, legal systems worldwide are striving to adapt. Some countries are exploring new regulations that recognize AI-assisted works while ensuring human creators retain their rights. Future developments in AI copyright law may include:

- **New legislation** explicitly defining AI-generated content ownership.
- **Hybrid copyright models** where AI and human collaboration are legally acknowledged.
- **AI ethics guidelines** to ensure responsible and fair use of generative models.

At this time, creators using AI in their work are advised to take steps to protect their intellectual property. This includes documenting their creative process, ensuring significant human involvement, and staying informed about evolving legal standards.

As AI's role in creativity expands, understanding legal considerations will be essential for artists, writers, musicians, and designers. By navigating these challenges thoughtfully, we can embrace AI's potential while safeguarding the rights and contributions of human creators.

Summary

As we have seen throughout this chapter, AI is reshaping creativity, making artistic expression more accessible while at the same time challenging ideas of originality and authorship. As this content becomes more prevalent, distinguishing between human and machine creation is becoming increasingly difficult. In the next chapter, we'll explore how to identify AI-generated works and their impact on digital authenticity.

8

IDENTIFYING AI-GENERATED CONTENT

Distinguishing between reality and AI-generated content is becoming increasingly difficult. With flawless execution and striking details, AI-generated imagery often blurs the line between the real and the artificial. This chapter explores the subtle yet telling signs that can help you identify AI-created visuals. By recognizing these key indicators, you'll be better equipped to assess the authenticity of the images you encounter.

SPOTTING AI-GENERATED IMAGES: KEY INDICATORS

One of the most common signs of AI-generated images is the presence of unnatural distortions. AI frequently struggles with rendering human hands correctly, sometimes adding extra fingers or misplaced joints—details that may go unnoticed at first but become obvious upon closer inspection. For example, in the picture with the family at the computer, it may seem normal until you notice the girl's unnatural hand in the middle and the strange placement of the boy's fingers on the mouse.

Another indicator of AI-generated imagery is the composition of the image itself. Symmetry, while pleasing to the eye, can sometimes be too perfect, especially in natural settings. AI tends to create repetitive elements in complex scenes, resulting in an uncanny uniformity. For example, trees in a forest might exhibit identical branch patterns or leaf arrangements, which is rare in nature. This repetition can serve as a red flag, suggesting that the image may not be entirely genuine.

Image quality is another facet where AI-generated content often falters. Despite their overall impressive appearance, these images frequently suffer from quality issues like blurring and edge distortions. You might notice blurred edges in detailed images, particularly around complex shapes or fast-moving subjects, which can detract from the overall sharpness of the scene. In portraits, facial features might appear distorted, with eyes misaligned or teeth unnaturally arranged, betraying the image's artificial origins. These quality issues arise from the limitations of current AI technology, which still faces challenges in replicating the intricate details of real-world visuals.

Use this list of common indicators to help determine whether an image has been generated by AI:

- **Distorted Hands and Fingers** – AI often struggles to render hands correctly, sometimes adding extra fingers, misplaced joints, or unnatural shapes.
- **Inconsistent or Impossible Backgrounds** – Objects may appear structurally improbable, such as misaligned architecture, warped landscapes, or oddly sized elements that disrupt natural composition.
- **Uncanny Symmetry and Repetition** – AI-generated images may exhibit perfect symmetry in natural

scenes or repetitive elements, such as trees with identical branches or patterns that feel unnatural.

- **Overly Smooth or Unnatural Faces** – Some AI-generated faces look too flawless, with perfect symmetry, blurred or plastic-like skin textures, or inconsistencies in facial features.
- **Blurring and Edge Distortions** – AI images may suffer from quality issues like blurred edges around complex shapes, unnatural blending, or inconsistencies in fine details.
- **Odd Lighting and Reflections** – AI can struggle with realistic shadows, reflections in mirrors, and consistent light sources, leading to unnatural or conflicting effects.
- **Jumbled or Incoherent Text** – Words on signs, book covers, or clothing often appear garbled or nonsensical, as AI struggles with accurate text rendering.

UNDERSTANDING DEEPFAKES AND THEIR IMPLICATIONS

Deepfakes represent a fascinating yet unsettling frontier, where AI technology is used to create hyper-realistic digital media that can mimic real people in videos and audio. This technology enables the creation of videos where a person's face is seamlessly superimposed onto another's body or where speech is generated to match this visual manipulation, producing media that is often indistinguishable from genuine footage. While deepfakes can be used for creative purposes, they also raise concerns about deception and misinformation.

Identifying deepfakes can be a challenging task, as they are designed to deceive viewers. However, certain characteristics can help you spot them. One common feature is inconsistent lip-syncing, where the movements of the mouth do not perfectly match the spoken words, creating a subtle but noticeable discord. Additionally, unnatural facial expressions or movements can betray a deepfake, as the technology sometimes struggles to replicate the nuanced expressions that naturally occur. You might notice that the eyes lack the natural liveliness you would expect, or that the head movements are slightly jerky or unnatural, breaking the illusion of authenticity.

The potential risks associated with deepfakes extend far beyond mere technical curiosity. They pose serious societal and ethical challenges, particularly in an era of growing public distrust in media. Political campaigns, for example, can exploit deepfakes to fabricate videos of public figures, spreading false narratives and manipulating public opinion. Beyond politics, deepfakes also raise concerns about personal privacy, as unauthorized likenesses can be used for identity theft, reputational harm, or fraud. Imagine a scenario where someone's face is superimposed onto inappropriate content or used in a scam—such violations can have profound personal and professional consequences, damaging relationships, careers, and even personal safety.

STAYING AHEAD: THE FUTURE OF AI CONTENT DETECTION

AI is advancing rapidly, generating images, videos, and text with increasing realism. As its capabilities improve, distinguishing between AI-generated and human-made content will only become more challenging. While this raises concerns about deception and fraud, it also opens up new possibilities for creative and productive uses.

To keep pace with AI's growth, detection methods are evolving. Some systems use AI itself to identify patterns in AI-generated content, scanning for inconsistencies that might escape the human eye. Others analyze metadata—hidden details in digital files that can reveal when and how they were created. Researchers are also studying micro-expressions, breathing patterns, and motion consistency to refine methods for detecting AI-generated videos.

Advanced detection tools include AI-powered systems like Deepware Scanner and Microsoft's Video Authenticator, which analyze videos and images for subtle signs of manipulation or AI generation. These tools look for pixel-level inconsistencies that may not be obvious to the human eye. Metadata analysis using forensic tools like FotoForensics can also uncover hidden information, such as software used or discrepancies in timestamps, which may signal AI generation. Reverse image search tools such as Google Reverse Image Search and TinEye can track the origin of an image and determine whether it has appeared elsewhere, offering additional support in verifying content.

One approach to maintaining transparency is watermarking AI-generated content. Some companies are embedding invisible digital markers in AI-created images, videos, and text to distinguish them from human-made content. While this won't prevent AI's misuse, it provides a way to track and verify its origins, making AI-generated content easier to manage responsibly. Additionally, behavioral analysis tools that examine micro-expressions, facial movements, and body language in videos can help identify AI-generated figures, as they often exhibit unnatural patterns that differ from real human behavior. Tools like Sensity AI focus on detecting these inconsistencies, particularly in facial features, to identify deepfake content.

Beyond technology, digital literacy remains essential. Understanding how AI works and developing strong critical thinking skills can help you evaluate what you see online. Checking sources, identifying inconsistencies, and recognizing potential manipulation can provide context rather than simply assuming content is either trustworthy or deceptive.

Summary

While technology continues to evolve, so too must our strategies for understanding and adapting to its impact. As AI continues to blur the lines between human and machine-created media, distinguishing real from fake will become harder. In many cases, it may not matter if you can tell an image is AI-generated—such as when a business uses AI to design a logo, a game developer creates background scenery, or a marketer designs social media visuals. But other times, it's crucial to know the difference. Scammers create fake profiles, deepfakes spread false information, and AI-generated news stories can mislead the public. Staying informed, thinking critically, and using verification tools are essential for navigating this landscape. With this in mind, the next chapter explores common challenges posed by AI and offers practical solutions to address them.

9

OVERCOMING COMMON CHALLENGES WITH AI

The first time humans harnessed fire, it was both terrifying and transformative. AI is no different—its power can be intimidating, but learning to control and apply it wisely unlocks immense potential. Fear, complacency, and over-reliance are three common pitfalls when adapting to AI's rise. Some resist change, others passively consume AI without deeper engagement, and many lean too heavily on its capabilities. This chapter provides a guide to navigating AI with confidence—overcoming fear, staying proactive in learning, and ensuring AI remains a tool that enhances human ingenuity rather than replacing it.

THE FEAR OF AI

For many, the world of AI can seem like an expansive and intimidating frontier. The rapid advancements and profound capabilities of AI often spark fear and uncertainty, especially among those new to the technology. You might worry about machines taking over jobs or invading personal privacy—concerns that are valid and widespread. The constant news cycle about AI breakthroughs can amplify these fears, making it feel like automation is accelerating beyond our control. Headlines about deepfake technology, AI surveillance, and ethical dilemmas can heighten anxiety, leaving many unsure about how AI will shape their future.

Yet, amidst these worries, it is equally important to recognize the transformative benefits of AI. The technology has already made significant strides in areas like healthcare, enhancing diagnostics and enabling earlier disease detection, ultimately saving lives. AI also helps eliminate many tedious and mundane tasks, allowing professionals to engage in more meaningful, creative, and strategic work. Beyond the workplace, AI's ability to save time helps reduce stress by easing workloads, allowing for more quality time with family and friends. Additionally, it enhances accessibility, offering tools like real-time language translation and assistive technologies that help break down communication barriers and empower individuals with disabilities. The difficulty lies in cutting through the noise, understanding the reality behind the headlines, and learning how AI can be leveraged as an asset rather than a source of fear.

Embracing this technology requires an open and adaptable mindset—one that is eager to learn, realistic about AI's continued progress, and accepts its enduring role in our lives. The digital landscape is changing rapidly, and those who adapt are the ones who thrive. Ignoring or resisting AI won't stop its progress, but learning to work with it can open doors to new opportunities. In this environment, lifelong learning is not just beneficial but essential. By continuously updating skills and embracing new technologies, you are positioning yourself to benefit from AI's advancements rather than being displaced by them. An open mind will allow you to see AI's potential to enhance creativity, efficiency, and productivity across various aspects of life. It encourages curiosity and the willingness to explore how the technology can complement human abilities, making tasks more manageable and enjoyable.

Education is a powerful antidote to fear. By exploring reliable resources, courses, and guides, you can develop a clear and practical understanding of AI. Numerous books, online courses, and interactive tutorials break down complex concepts into manageable lessons, making AI accessible to learners at any level. Universities, tech organizations, and industry leaders provide both free and paid educational materials, from beginner-friendly introductions to advanced technical training. This book serves as a valuable starting point, equipping you with foundational knowledge, practical applications, and the confidence to integrate AI into your life. With the right mindset and resources, learning AI becomes an empowering journey rather than an overwhelming challenge.

COMPLACENCY IN LEARNING

One of the biggest hurdles in learning AI isn't mastering complex algorithms or coding—it's simply getting started. Many people hesitate to dive in because they assume it's too complicated, too technical, or only for experts with advanced degrees in math and computer science. This couldn't be further from the truth. AI is more accessible than ever, with intuitive tools that allow anyone to experiment, automate tasks, and integrate AI into their daily lives without needing to understand the underlying mechanics. The key is to take that first step—whether it's trying out an AI-powered productivity tool, exploring a no-code machine learning platform, or reading about real-world applications. The biggest obstacle to learning AI is often the belief that it's too difficult to begin.

However, complacency doesn't just affect beginners—it can also set in once people have started using AI. With so many user-friendly platforms available, it's easy to become a passive consumer, relying on AI tools without truly exploring their full potential. Many people stop at using AI for simple tasks like summarizing text, generating ideas, or automating routine work, without pushing further to see how it could enhance their creativity, decision-making, or problem-solving skills. While AI can handle a lot on its own, the real power comes from those who actively engage with it —experimenting, questioning, and adapting the technology to fit their specific needs.

Another reason complacency takes hold is the assumption that AI has reached its peak. Some people believe that because advanced models like ChatGPT or image-generation tools already exist, there's little left to learn. This mindset is a mistake. AI is continuing to evolve rapidly, and each year brings new breakthroughs in automation, personalization, and problem-solving. Those who keep up with these advancements will have a competitive edge, whether in business, education, research, or creative fields. The biggest risk isn't AI replacing human jobs—it's people failing to adapt to the opportunities AI creates.

To avoid falling into complacency, the key is to stay curious and engaged. One of the best ways to do this is by applying AI to real-world challenges. Instead of just consuming AI-generated content, try using AI to automate a repetitive task, brainstorm new ideas, or enhance a personal or professional project. Joining AI communities, attending meetups, and participating in discussions can also help keep motivation high. Setting small, achievable learning goals—such as exploring a new AI tool every month or following industry trends—can make the process feel less overwhelming.

Ultimately, learning AI should be seen as an ongoing journey, not a one-time effort. The more you explore and experiment, the more AI becomes a powerful force for innovation, creativity, and productivity. Whether you're a beginner or looking to expand your expertise, the key is to keep progressing. The real challenge isn't mastering AI—it's hesitating to begin or giving up too soon.

OVER-RELIANCE ON AI

While complacency is a major challenge in learning and using AI, the opposite extreme can be just as problematic—becoming overly reliant on technology and AI. As AI tools grow more powerful and accessible, it's easy to rely on them increasingly, often without questioning their accuracy or appreciating the importance of human insight. AI's convenience can create a subtle yet profound shift—rather than using it to boost productivity and creativity, some rely on it as a crutch, letting it make decisions, shape opinions, and even replace their own problem-solving abilities.

This over-reliance on AI can be seen in many areas. In writing and content creation, AI-generated text can speed up the process, but if used without thoughtful oversight, it can produce generic, uninspired work that lacks a personal touch. In decision-making, AI-driven analytics can provide valuable insights, but blind trust in algorithmic recommendations without human judgment can lead to biased or flawed conclusions. Even in everyday life, from using AI-powered assistants to relying on recommendation algorithms for news and entertainment, the risk of passively accepting AI's suggestions without critical thinking is real.

The key to using AI effectively is balance—leveraging its strengths while maintaining human oversight, creativity, and independent thinking. AI is a powerful assistant, but it should never replace human intuition, ethical reasoning, or the ability to question and adapt. The best approach is to use AI as a collaborator rather than a decision-maker, treating its outputs as suggestions rather than absolute answers.

A balanced approach also means knowing when to step away from AI. Not every problem needs an automated solution, and not every creative task should be outsourced to a machine. There is value in doing things manually—whether it's writing, brainstorming, problem-solving, or making complex decisions—because it strengthens critical thinking and deepens understanding. As we have discussed throughout this book, AI should enhance human capabilities, not replace them.

Ultimately, AI is most effective when used in partnership with human intelligence. It can provide efficiency, insight, and automation, but real innovation comes from the combination of AI's capabilities and human creativity, intuition, and ethical awareness. The goal is not to let AI do everything for us, but to use it in a way that enhances our abilities while keeping us actively engaged in the process. Striking this balance ensures that AI remains an asset, rather than a dependency.

Summary

Adapting to AI isn't about mastering every technical detail—it's about developing the mindset to learn, experiment, and evolve alongside it. The key is to stay informed, use AI thoughtfully, and know when to rely on human judgment. Those who approach AI with curiosity and adaptability will find the greatest opportunities. In the next and final chapter, we'll put everything you've learned into action with practical exercises and step-by-step guidance to help you start using AI in meaningful, hands-on ways.

10

INTERACTIVE EXERCISES: PUT KNOWLEDGE INTO ACTION

Now that you've learned the fundamentals of AI, it's time to put that knowledge into action. Understanding AI conceptually is one thing, but experiencing its power firsthand is where the real learning happens. The best way to become comfortable with AI is through hands-on experimentation—trying different tools, testing their capabilities, and seeing how they can enhance your daily tasks in practical ways.

By applying AI to real-world situations, you'll gain tangible experience that reinforces what you've learned. You don't need to be a tech expert or a programmer to take advantage of these tools—many are designed to be intuitive, user-friendly, and accessible to anyone. Whether you want to save time, boost efficiency, or simply explore AI's potential, the key is to start with tools that deliver immediate benefits.

This chapter includes five hands-on exercises with step-by-step guides to help you experience AI in action. These exercises walk you through practical applications of AI, allowing you to build confidence while discovering how these tools can simplify everyday tasks and enhance productivity. You can choose the exercises that interest you most or explore them all—it's entirely up to you.

Here's a preview of the five hands-on exercises you'll be working through:

1. **Smarter Note-Taking**: Capture and summarize conversations with Otter.ai.
2. **AI-Powered Shopping Assistance**: Identify and find products with Google Lens.
3. **AI-Powered Presentations**: Design professional slides effortlessly with Gamma.
4. **AI Image Creation**: Generate stunning visuals in seconds with DALL-E.
5. **Effortless Translation**: Break language barriers using DeepL.

Each exercise includes detailed instructions, making it easy to follow along and try these AI tools for yourself. Plus, you'll find recommendations for similar tools, giving you more options to explore and find the AI-powered solution that works best for your needs. Best of all, every example in this chapter features free ways to experiment with AI, so you can test these tools without any cost or commitment.

The more you explore, the better you'll understand AI's potential and how it can seamlessly integrate into your workflow.

Let's dive in and start bringing AI to life!

SMARTER NOTE-TAKING WITH OTTER.AI

Traditional note-taking can be time-consuming and prone to missed details, making it difficult to keep up during meetings, lectures, and brainstorming sessions. AI-powered transcription tools like Otter.ai eliminate this hassle by automatically converting speech into text, organizing notes, and highlighting key takeaways—allowing you to stay focused and engaged while capturing every important detail. By leveraging AI, note-taking becomes more efficient, accurate, and stress-free—helping you focus on the conversation instead of scrambling to keep up.

Advantages of AI-powered transcription tools:

- Real-Time Transcription – Get instant text as people speak.
- Searchable Notes – Quickly find key points by searching keywords.
- Speaker Identification – Easily distinguish who said what.
- Automatic Summarization – AI highlights key takeaways for quick review.

- Sync Across Devices – Access your notes anywhere, anytime.

Example Exercise

Set up a brief 20-minute meeting with 1–3 friends, family members, or colleagues—either in person or virtually. The goal is to simulate a real discussion and test how well AI transcribes the conversation. Choose a simple, engaging topic that everyone can comfortably discuss, such as:

- How can AI help in our daily lives?
- Best productivity hacks we use at work/school.
- Brainstorming ideas for our next group project/event.

Before the meeting, sign up for Otter.ai and choose the free plan, which allows you to transcribe up to 300 minutes per month, with a 30-minute limit per conversation. Make sure to explore the Otter.ai dashboard in advance so you're familiar with its features and can smoothly record and transcribe your discussion.

Follow these steps to record, transcribe, and analyze your discussion using Otter.ai:

1. **Log into Otter.ai and choose one of these options:**
    - Live Recording: Click the "Record" button to transcribe in real-time.

    - Zoom Integration (optional): If using Zoom, enable Otter.ai's integration to automatically capture audio.
2. **Allow microphone access when prompted**
3. **Let Otter.ai run while you discuss your topic naturally**
    - Speak clearly, or place your device near the speaker during a meeting or lecture.
4. **Edit and organize your transcript**
    - Click on the transcript to make manual edits if needed.
    - Assign speaker names for clarity.
    - Highlight important sections or add comments.
5. **Save, share, or export your notes**
    - Click the three-dot menu next to the transcript to share it with colleagues.
    - Export the transcript as a TXT, PDF, or DOCX file for easy reference.
    - Revisit your notes anytime by logging into your Otter.ai account.

Alternative AI Note-Taking Tools

If you're looking for alternatives to Otter.ai for meeting notes, consider these AI-powered tools:

- **Fireflies.ai**: Integrates with Zoom, Microsoft Teams, and Google Meet, automatically recording and summarizing key discussions.

- **Jamie**: An AI-powered meeting assistant that creates structured summaries, making it easy to extract action items.
- **Fathom**: Provides automatic meeting transcription with highlights and integrates with major conferencing platforms.

IDENTIFY AND FIND PRODUCTS WITH GOOGLE LENS

Shopping has never been easier, thanks to AI-powered tools like Google Lens. Instead of struggling to describe an item in a search bar—especially when shopping for unique or hard-to-name products like clothing, furniture, or accessories—simply scan it to instantly identify, compare prices, or find similar alternatives. This is particularly useful for discovering deals, locating out-of-stock products, and even translating product labels in different languages. By analyzing images on the spot, Google Lens streamlines the shopping experience, saving time and ensuring smarter, more informed purchasing decisions.

Advantages of AI-powered shopping tools:

- Instant Product Recognition – Simply snap a photo of an item to get instant search results.
- Price Comparisons – Find the best deals across multiple online retailers.

- Alternative Suggestions – Discover similar products in different styles or price ranges.
- Easy Barcode Scanning – Quickly access product details by scanning barcodes.
- Find Items You See in Real Life – No need to guess brand names, just point your camera at a product.

Example Exercise

The next time you're in a store, give Google Lens a try. Simply open the app, point your smartphone camera at the product, and let AI do the work. In seconds, Google Lens will identify the item, provide pricing details from various retailers, and suggest alternative options. It can even help with out-of-stock products by directing you to similar items. All you need is your phone and a product you're curious about.

Follow these steps to see Google Lens in action:

1. **Pick an Item to Identify**
    - Look around for an interesting item you'd like to find online. Here are some ideas: a pair of shoes you've been admiring, a backpack or handbag in a different color, or a piece of furniture you saw in a store but want to compare prices on.
2. **Open Google Lens**
    - On Android, open your Camera app or the Google app and tap the Lens icon.

   - On iPhone, open the Google app and select Lens from the search bar.
3. **Scan or Upload a Photo**
   - Point your camera at the item and tap the search button.
   - If you already have a picture (e.g., a screenshot from social media), upload it to Google Lens.
4. **Check the Results**
   - See if Google Lens correctly identifies the product.
   - Look through the search results to find online stores, prices, and reviews.
5. **Compare and Explore**
   - If the exact product is available, compare prices across different stores.
   - If not, check similar products in different styles or price ranges.
   - Try scanning a few different objects to see how well Google Lens performs.

Bonus tip – Google Lens isn't just for online shopping. It can help in other real-world situations, such as:

- Identify Fashion Items – Spot a stylish outfit and find where to buy it.
- Find Books and Reviews – Scan a book cover to read reviews and purchase it online.

- Search for Home Décor – Scan furniture or decorations to find similar styles.
- Identify Artwork – Discover artists and purchase prints of artwork you like.
- Scan Food and Menus – Find recipes by scanning ingredients or restaurant dishes.

Alternative AI Shopping Tools

If you're looking for additional AI-powered shopping assistants, consider:

- **Amazon StyleSnap**: Upload a photo to find similar clothing on Amazon.
- **Pinterest Lens**: Discover ideas and shopping options from Pinterest's vast collection.
- **Bing Visual Search**: A Microsoft-powered tool for finding products through image searches.

DESIGN PROFESSIONAL SLIDES EFFORTLESSLY WITH GAMMA

Creating engaging and visually appealing presentations no longer requires hours of formatting or advanced design skills. Traditional slide design can be tedious and often demands an understanding of design principles to create polished, professional-looking slides. AI-powered tools like Gamma simplify the process by automatically generating well-structured, aesthetically pleasing presentations with minimal effort. These tools not only save time but also ensure high-quality results, allowing you to focus on delivering your message rather than struggling with layouts and formatting.

Advantages of AI-powered presentation tools:

- Instant Slide Creation – Generate polished presentations in minutes.
- Smart Formatting – AI automatically arranges text, images, and layouts for a cohesive design.
- No Design Experience Needed – Easily create professional slides without prior design skills.
- Customizable Themes – Choose from various styles to match your brand or topic.
- Interactive and Responsive – Add dynamic elements like videos, links, and animations effortlessly.

Example Exercise

For this exercise, choose a topic that is both informative and engaging, such as health, productivity, travel, or history. Select your own topic or choose from one of the following suggested themes:

- The Science of Sleep: Why It's Important and How to Improve It
- Mastering Memory: Proven Strategies to Learn Faster and Retain More

- The Benefits of Mindfulness and Meditation
- How to Plan the Perfect Budget-Friendly Trip

Once you've selected a topic, use Gamma to generate a well-structured presentation. The AI will help create an outline, suggest content, and format slides automatically, allowing you to focus on refining the information and visuals. After finalizing your presentation, share it with a friend, colleague, or family member, gather feedback, and reflect on how AI streamlined the process while still allowing for personalization.

Follow these steps to design your first AI-powered presentation with Gamma:

1. **Sign Up for Gamma**
   - Visit gamma.app and create a free account.
   - Explore the available templates and AI-assisted features.
2. **Generate Your Slides**
   - "Create new" presentation.
   - Choose the option to "Generate" and enter your selected topic.
   - Review and edit the proposed outline.
   - "Generate" your presentation.
3. **Customize and Enhance**
   - Choose a theme and layout that best fits your presentation style.

    - Edit text, rearrange slides, or add images, icons, and charts with AI-powered suggestions.
    - Use interactive features like embedded videos and live links to enhance engagement.
4. **Share and Present**
    - Preview your slides and make final adjustments.
    - Share your presentation via a link or download it as a PDF.
    - Present directly from Gamma, which offers a scroll-based, non-linear experience for seamless navigation.

Bonus tip – Gamma isn't just for traditional slides. It can help create various types of presentations, such as:

- Business Reports – Generate professional decks for meetings and proposals.
- Educational Content – Create interactive lesson slides for teaching.
- Pitch Decks – Design compelling startup or investor pitches.
- Data Visualizations – Present complex data with auto-formatted charts and graphs.
- Social Media Storytelling – Build engaging presentations for sharing online.

Alternative AI-Powered Presentation Tools

If you want to explore more AI-assisted presentation tools, consider:

- **Beautiful.ai**: AI-powered design for stunning, modern presentations.
- **Tome**: A storytelling-focused AI tool for creating visually rich decks.
- **Canva Magic Design**: AI-assisted templates for presentations and social media graphics.

CREATING IMAGES WITH DALL-E

Creating stunning visuals no longer requires costly software, advanced skills, or hours of work. Tools like DALL-E generate high-quality images from simple text descriptions in seconds, streamlining the design process. AI-powered tools eliminate the need for expertise, allowing anyone to produce professional visuals for presentations, marketing, social media, and creative projects. Plus, DALL-E now integrates with ChatGPT, making it even easier to generate and customize images with just a few prompts.

Advantages of AI-powered image generators:

- Instant Generation – Create unique visuals in seconds with a simple text prompt.

- Customizable Styles – Experiment with different art styles, from realistic photography to digital painting.
- No Design Experience Needed – Anyone can create professional-looking images without prior artistic skills.
- Versatile Use Cases – Ideal for presentations, social media content, personal projects, and more.

Example Exercise

Follow these steps to generate your first AI image using DALL-E:

1. **Sign Up for DALL-E**
    - Visit openai.com/dall-e and create a free OpenAI account.
    - Log in and check your free credit balance, which allows you to generate images without cost.
    - Note: If you have the paid version of ChatGPT, you can use DALL-E to generate and edit images by providing text prompts directly within the chat.
2. **Generate and Refine Your Image**
    - Think of a creative and descriptive prompt. The more details you provide, the better the results. Example: "A futuristic cityscape at sunset, with flying cars and glowing neon signs."
    - Enter your prompt into DALL-E's text box and click "Generate."

   - Review the generated image.
   - If needed, refine your prompt by adding specific details (e.g., colors, lighting, atmosphere).
3. **Experiment with Different Styles**
   - Realistic photography: "A high-resolution photo of a golden retriever sitting in a field of tulips."
   - Cartoon illustration: "A hand-drawn comic-style superhero flying over a city skyline."
   - Fantasy art: "A glowing enchanted forest with tiny fairy houses in the trees."
4. **Save and Use Your Image**
   - Download your favorite creation.
   - Use it for blog posts, social media, presentations, or creative projects.

Alternative AI Image Generators

If you're looking for alternatives to DALL-E, consider these AI-powered tools:

- **Deep Dream Generator:** A deep-learning-based tool that applies unique artistic styles to images.
- **Stable Diffusion**: Open-source AI for generating highly detailed and customizable images.
- **Runway ML:** AI-powered creative tools designed for artists and designers.

BREAK LANGUAGE BARRIERS USING DEEPL

Language no longer has to be a barrier to communication, thanks to AI-powered translation tools like DeepL. These tools offer fast, accurate translations that help individuals and businesses communicate seamlessly across multiple languages. Advanced AI models ensure translations sound more natural and contextually accurate, making them ideal for emails, reports, travel, and everyday conversations. DeepL's free version lets users translate up to 1,500 characters per request. Users can also translate up to three documents per month, each up to 5 MB, in formats like Microsoft Word, PowerPoint, and PDF.

Advantages of using AI for language translation:

- High-Quality Translations – AI-powered translation tools provide more natural, context-aware translations compared to traditional machine translation.
- Supports Multiple Languages – Many AI tools offer translation for dozens of languages.
- Fast and Easy to Use – Instantly translate text, documents, or even entire web pages with just a few clicks.
- Enhances Accessibility – Bridges language gaps in education, business, and travel, making information more widely available.

Example Exercise

DeepL is a user-friendly AI-powered translation tool that makes translating text and documents quick and effortless. Whether you need to translate individual words and phrases or entire documents, DeepL's intuitive interface ensures a seamless experience.

Following these steps to practice using DeepL for both quick translations and full document translations:

1. **Using DeepL for Quick Word and Phrase Translations**
    - Go to DeepL.com and open the translation tool.
    - Type individual words or sentences in your native language into the text box.
    - Select a target language and translate the text.
    - Reverse the process by translating the results back into your original language.
    - Compare for accuracy and note any differences.
    - Use DeepL's alternative suggestions to refine phrasing and improve sentence structure.
2. **Translating a Full Document While Preserving Formatting**
    - Choose a document (less than 5 MB), such as a business report, research paper, or article.
    - Go to DeepL.com and click on "Translate files."
    - Create a free account if you don't already have one.

- Upload your document to the translation tool.
- Select the target language for translation.
- Translate the document—DeepL will preserve formatting, including headings, bullet points, and layout.
- Review the translated text for accuracy and natural flow.

Alternative AI Translation Tools

If you're looking for alternatives to DeepL for AI-powered translations, consider these tools:

- **Google Translate**: A widely used translation tool that supports over 130 languages, offering text, voice, image, and real-time website translations.
- **Microsoft Translator**: Provides AI-driven translations for text, speech, and documents, with seamless integration into Microsoft Office and Teams.
- **Amazon Translate**: A cloud-based AI translation service designed for businesses, offering real-time and batch translations for websites and apps.
- **Lingvanex:** An AI-powered translator with support for offline translation, voice recognition, and integration with chat applications.

CONCLUSION

As we come to the end of our journey through the world of AI, I hope you now see that AI is not some distant, complex technology reserved for experts. Instead, it is a powerful, accessible tool that you can harness to enhance your daily life, boost productivity, and unlock new possibilities. Throughout this book, we've explored the fundamental concepts of this technology, from machine learning and neural networks to natural language processing, and discovered how these seemingly complex ideas can be distilled into simple, practical applications.

We've seen how AI seamlessly integrates into your everyday routine, transforming your smartphone into a personal assistant, your home into a smart haven, and your fitness tracker into a health guru. From managing your finances to planning your meals, AI is there to simplify tasks and free up your time for what truly matters. The step-by-step guides we've provided empower you to adopt AI tools like Grammarly, virtual assistants, and other productivity tools with ease, unlocking their potential to revolutionize the way you work and create.

Our deep dive into ChatGPT showcased the incredible versatility of this AI powerhouse. You now have the knowledge to craft effective prompts and leverage the platform for a variety of tasks. The real-world examples we explored across healthcare, retail, education, and entertainment demonstrate the transformative impact of AI in various industries, highlighting its potential to drive innovation and improve lives.

As you embark on your own AI journey, remember the importance of responsible usage and data protection. The ethical challenges and privacy concerns we explored highlight the importance of approaching AI with mindfulness and integrity. By staying informed and adopting best practices, you can navigate the landscape with confidence and contribute to shaping a future where AI benefits all.

The productivity-enhancing tools and techniques we covered, from streamlining communication to automating repetitive tasks, are now at your fingertips. Use the opportunity to streamline your workflow and create more mental space for creativity and strategic thinking. Speaking of creativity, I encourage you to explore AI's potential in the arts, music, writing, and design. Collaborating with this technology really does open up new avenues for self-expression and pushes the boundaries of what's possible.

As you continue to engage with AI, stay curious about emerging trends like generative AI and its implications for the future. The ability to identify AI-generated content is a valuable skill in an era where distinguishing between the real and the synthetic becomes increasingly challenging. Armed with the strategies and tools we discussed, you can now approach AI with a critical eye and make informed judgments.

If you ever find yourself hesitating or feeling overwhelmed, remember the strategies we explored for overcoming fears, avoiding complacency, and maintaining balance. The AI community is here to support you, offering resources, inspiration, and opportunities for lifelong learning. Embrace the future with an open mind, knowing that your adaptability and willingness to learn are your greatest assets.

As I conclude this book, my hope is that you feel empowered and excited about the possibilities AI holds for you. The knowledge and insights you've gained are your toolkit for thriving in an AI-driven world. So, go forth and experiment with the tools and concepts we've covered. Apply them to your own life, and witness the transformative power of AI firsthand. Join communities of like-minded learners, and continue to grow your understanding of this fascinating field.

Keep in mind, AI is here not to replace you, but to empower you. It is a tool that amplifies your potential and helps you achieve more than you ever thought possible. So, embrace it with curiosity, confidence, and a commitment to using it for good. The future is yours to shape, and with AI by your side, there are no limits to what you can accomplish.

REFERENCES

AIVA. (n.d.). AI-generated music composition and orchestration. Retrieved from https://www.aiva.ai

Adobe. (n.d.). AI in digital media: The future of content creation. Retrieved from https://www.adobe.com

Adobe. (n.d.). Adobe Sensei: AI-powered creative tools. Retrieved from https://www.adobe.com/sensei.html

AI Addiction in Adults: Addressing Dependency in the Intelligence Age. (n.d.). Hyper Policy. Retrieved from https://hyperpolicy.org/insights/ai-addiction-in-adults-addressing-dependency-in-the-intelligence-age/

AI Budgeting Tools: Personal Finance Management. (n.d.). SoFi. Retrieved from https://www.sofi.com/learn/content/ai-budgeting-tools/

AI for Project Management: Tools and Best Practices. (n.d.). Atlassian. Retrieved from https://www.atlassian.com/work-management/project-management/ai-project-management

Amper Music. (n.d.). AI-assisted music creation for artists and composers. Retrieved from https://www.ampermusic.com

Artificial Intelligence and the Erosion of Human Social Skills. (n.d.). Medium. Retrieved from https://medium.com/neuranest/artificial-intelligence-and-the-erosion-of-human-social-skills-82772f06772a

Artificial Intelligence for Medical Diagnostics—Existing and Future. (n.d.). PubMed Central. Retrieved from https://pmc.ncbi.nlm.nih.gov/articles/PMC9955430/#:~:text=AI%20can%20analyze%20large%20amounts,history%2C%20and%20laboratory%20test%20results.

Brynjolfsson, E., & McAfee, A. (2017). *Machine, platform, crowd: Harnessing our digital future.* W. W. Norton & Company.

Canva. (n.d.). AI-driven design assistance and graphic creation. Retrieved from https://www.canva.com

Coursera. (n.d.). AI education for beginners and non-technical users. Retrieved from https://www.coursera.org

DALL-E. (n.d.). Text-to-image generation with AI. OpenAI. Retrieved from https://openai.com/dall-e

DeepArt.io. (n.d.). AI-powered image generation and style transfer. Retrieved from https://deepart.io

DeepL. (n.d.). DeepL Translator. Retrieved from https://www.deepl.com

DeepMind. (2023). The role of artificial intelligence in healthcare diagnostics. Retrieved from https://deepmind.com

Deepfake Detection Lab. (n.d.). Detecting AI-generated media through advanced forensic analysis. Retrieved from https://www.deepfakedetection.org

Deepware Scanner. (n.d.). Deepware Scanner: AI video manipulation detection tool. Retrieved from https://www.deepware.ai

Domingos, P. (2015). *The master algorithm: How the quest for the ultimate learning machine will remake our world*. Basic Books.

Delivering on the Promise of AI to Improve Health Outcomes. (2023, December 14). The White House. Retrieved from https://www.whitehouse.gov/briefing-room/blog/2023/12/14/delivering-on-the-promise-of-ai-to-improve-health-outcomes/

FamiSafe. (n.d.). FamiSafe: The ultimate family safety app. Retrieved February 25, 2025, from https://www.famisafe.com

Ford, M. (2015). *Rise of the robots: Technology and the threat of a jobless future*. Basic Books.

FotoForensics. (n.d.). FotoForensics: Image forensics and analysis. Retrieved from https://www.fotoforensics.com

Gamma. (n.d.). Create presentations effortlessly with AI. Retrieved from https://www.gamma.app

Garfinkel, S. (2021). *The computer book: From the abacus to artificial intelligence, 250 milestones in the history of computer science*. Sterling.

Google AI. (n.d.). Machine learning and AI in visual creativity. Retrieved from https://ai.google/research

Google AI. (n.d.). Machine learning in content authenticity and deepfake detection. Retrieved from https://ai.google/research

Google AI. (n.d.). Teachable Machine: No-code AI experimentation. Retrieved from https://teachablemachine.withgoogle.com

Google Lens. (n.d.). AI-powered shopping and image recognition tool. Retrieved from https://lens.google

Haenlein, M., & Kaplan, A. (2019). A brief history of artificial intelligence: On the past, present, and future of artificial intelligence. *California Management Review, 61*(4), 5-14. https://doi.org/10.1177/0008125619864925

How Grammarly Uses AI to Revolutionize Writing Assistance. (n.d.). 923. Retrieved from https://www.ninetwothree.co/blog/how-grammarly-uses-ai-to-revolutionize-writing-assistance

Is Society Ready for the Impact of AI on the Workforce? (n.d.). *CIGI*. Retrieved from https://www.cigionline.org/articles/is-society-ready-for-the-impact-of-ai-on-the-workforce/

Kayak. (2025). Kayak: AI-driven vacation planning and booking. Kayak. https://www.kayak.com

Marcus, G. (2022). *Rebooting AI: Building artificial intelligence we can trust*. Pantheon.

Midjourney. (n.d.). AI-generated imagery for digital artists. Retrieved from https://www.midjourney.com

MIT Media Lab. (n.d.). Deepfake technology and misinformation in digital media. Retrieved from https://www.media.mit.edu

MIT Technology Review. (n.d.). The impact of AI on the job market and workforce evolution. Retrieved from https://www.technologyreview.com

Mitchell, M. (2019). *Artificial intelligence: A guide for thinking humans*. Farrar, Straus and Giroux.

Motion. (2025). Motion: The AI-powered task manager. Motion. https://www.motionapp.com

Netflix. (n.d.). AI-driven recommendation systems and personalized content delivery. Retrieved from https://about.netflix.com

Non-Technical Introduction to AI Fundamentals. (n.d.). NetGuru. Retrieved from https://www.netguru.com/blog/crash-course-introduction-to-ai-fundamentals

NVIDIA. (n.d.). AI-powered video synthesis and generative modeling. Retrieved from https://www.nvidia.com

OpenAI. (2023). ChatGPT and AI-assisted writing tools. Retrieved from https://openai.com/chatgpt

OpenAI. (2023). ChatGPT and AI's role in digital media generation. Retrieved from https://openai.com

OpenAI. (2023). Understanding AI's potential and addressing common misconceptions. Retrieved from https://openai.com

Otter.ai. (n.d.). AI-powered transcription tool for meetings and lectures. Retrieved from https://www.otter.ai

Revolutionizing Inventory Management: The Power of AI. (n.d.). Akkio. Retrieved from https://www.akkio.com/post/ai-for-inventory-management

Reuters. (n.d.). The rise of AI-generated deepfake videos and their impact on journalism. Retrieved from https://www.reuters.com

RunwayML. (n.d.). AI for creative professionals in video and design. Retrieved from https://runwayml.com

Russell, S., & Norvig, P. (2020). *Artificial intelligence: A modern approach* (4th ed.). Pearson.

Smith, B. (2019). *Tools and weapons: The promise and the peril of the digital age*. Penguin Press.

Sony CSL Research Laboratory. (n.d.). AI-driven music generation and composition. Retrieved from https://www.sonycsl.co.jp

Sudowrite. (n.d.). AI-powered creative writing assistance. Retrieved from https://www.sudowrite.com

Tegmark, M. (2017). *Life 3.0: Being human in the age of artificial intelligence*. Knopf.

The Basics of Neural Networks: Explained Using Pizza Analogy. (n.d.). Medium. Retrieved from https://medium.com/@kirtankarvaibhav24/the-basics-of-neural-networks-explained-using-pizza-analogy-f685da3d3abb

Todoist. (2025). Todoist: AI to-do list manager for smarter task management. Todoist. https://www.todoist.com

Udemy. (n.d.). AI learning resources for beginners: Courses and structured pathways. Retrieved from https://www.udemy.com

University of Oxford, Centre for AI Ethics. (n.d.). Ethical

considerations in AI-generated content and misinformation. Retrieved from https://www.ox.ac.uk

West, D. M. (2018). *The future of work: Robots, AI, and automation*. Brookings Institution Press.

WIPO. (2023). AI and intellectual property: Navigating legal frameworks for AI-generated content. Retrieved from https://www.wipo.int

WIPO. (2023). Intellectual property and AI-generated media: Legal and ethical challenges. Retrieved from https://www.wipo.int

Wordtune. (n.d.). AI-driven writing enhancement and style refinement. Retrieved from https://www.wordtune.com

World Economic Forum. (2023). The future of work: AI's impact on employment and innovation. Retrieved from https://www.weforum.org

www.ingramcontent.com/pod-product-compliance
Lightning Source LLC
LaVergne TN
LVHW022048200926
848481LV00003B/823
* 9 7 9 8 3 4 9 2 5 5 1 6 8 *